THE BREAD BAKER'S COMPANION

BRIAN HART HOFFMAN

THE BREAD BAKER'S COMPANION

71 Recipes to Bake Better Bread at Home

83 press®

83 Press
2323 2nd Avenue North
Birmingham, Alabama 35203
83press.com

ISBN: 978-1-971708-09-6
Printed in China

CONTENTS

At the Heart of Bread

Bread is, for me, the most reassuring thing a kitchen can offer. It asks for very little and gives so much in return.

There are days when only a bold, crusty loaf will do, its crackle promising depth and drama. And then there are days—many of them—when what you want is softness. A yielding crumb. A hot biscuit waiting for a pat of butter and strawberry jam. The kind of bread that makes the house smell wonderful and the world feel kinder.

This book is an invitation to bake in that spirit. Bread here is not treated as a trial or a test but as a practice—something you return to because it gives comfort as much as sustenance. You'll find loaves that slip easily into everyday life alongside breads that ask you to linger a little longer, recipes that reassure rather than intimidate, written to guide you through the process with clarity and confidence. Bread, after all, is forgiving. It wants you to succeed.

There is a particular satisfaction in drawing bread from the oven—hot, fragrant, unmistakably yours. It is a pleasure that feels at once ordinary and profound, nourishing in every sense of the word.

This is bread as it should be: comforting, elemental, and made to be shared.

Preheat your oven; it's time to bake.

Brian

THE
CRUMB
TELLS
ALL

What Is Bread?

Bread is the result of structure, lift, and heat working together

At its simplest, bread is flour combined with liquid and leavening and then baked until its structure sets. What defines bread is not a single method or timeline but the way ingredients interact—how proteins form gluten, how gas is produced and trapped, and how heat fixes everything in place.

When flour is hydrated, its proteins link to form gluten, an elastic network that gives dough strength and extensibility. Leavening then creates gas, which expands within that network to produce volume and crumb. That leavening may come from yeast or from chemical agents such as baking powder and baking soda. The source of lift changes the process, but the goal is always the same: structure that can hold air.

From there, bread takes many forms. Lean breads rely on flour, water, salt, and fermentation for flavor and strength. Enriched breads include fats, sugars, eggs, or dairy, which soften gluten, slow fermentation, and produce a tender crumb. Rolls and pull-apart breads are shaped for portioning and softness, with structure designed to yield easily. Quick breads bypass fermentation entirely, using chemical leavening to create immediate lift and speed.

Bread-baking becomes far less intimidating once you understand the method. A dough behaves the way it does for a reason. Stickiness, slackness, slow fermentation, rapid rise—these are signals, not failures. Learning to read them is more useful than following instructions blindly.

This book is built to teach that understanding through clearly explained processes broken down into manageable steps. The aim is confidence—not just in following a recipe but also in knowing what to expect and how to adjust.

So, what is bread? It is gluten providing structure. It is leavening creating lift. It is heat setting the final form.

And once you understand that system, bread—in all its forms—becomes easier, more intuitive, and far more satisfying to make.

Essential Ingredients

Excellent baking requires wonderful ingredients. Here are the ingredients I use most often in my breads.

Flour: Quite simply, you cannot create bread without flour, and a key factor in choosing the right flour is knowing its protein level.

All-Purpose—As the name suggests, this flour works for most every type of bread. Made from a blend of hard and soft wheat with 10% to 11% protein, it creates moderate chew and tenderness. All-purpose flour is ideal for quick breads, cinnamon rolls, and other soft breads.

Bread—With 11% to 13% protein, this hard-wheat flour creates dough with significant chewiness and elasticity. It's best-suited for pretzels, baguettes, and intricately shaped breads.

Unbleached flours from esteemed mills such as Bob's Red Mill and King Arthur ensure a pure, robust base. These flours, free from chemical whitening agents, impart a natural, hearty flavor and contribute to the desired structure in your bakes.

Yeast: Yeast is a living organism, a fungus, that comes in multiple forms and needs proper care to produce the carbon dioxide needed to make bread rise.

Active Dry—This form of yeast comes in pellets made up of live yeast cells surrounded by dehydrated cells and a growth medium. Typically, recipes call for rehydrating, or proofing, it in warm water to activate the dormant yeast.

Instant—This form comes in smaller pellets that contain more live cells than active dry yeast. It can be added directly to dough or proofed in warm water. Its smaller shape and composition mean it activates more quickly than active dry yeast.

Sourdough Starter—Many people overlook sourdough starter as a form of yeast. In reality, this mixture of flour and water that is allowed to ferment naturally is the oldest known form. A live culture of yeast lives in the flour and water mixture you create, feed, and use. Bakers have been known to keep starters alive for decades.

Chemical Leavening Agents: Ensuring your baking soda and baking powder are fresh is essential for achieving the desired texture and rise in your quick breads. Store them in airtight containers in a cool, dry place to maintain their potency.

Before baking, test their effectiveness: Mix 1 teaspoon baking soda with 1 tablespoon (15 grams) vinegar; if it bubbles vigorously, it's active. Combine 1 teaspoon baking powder with ½ cup (120 grams) hot water; a strong fizz confirms it's still potent.

Regularly checking their "best by" dates and performing these simple tests will ensure your quick breads achieve their ideal rise and texture.

European-Style Butter: Butter is not merely a fat; it's a flavor carrier. European-style butters such as Kerrygold, Plugrà, and Président, with their higher butterfat content (around 82%), offer a richness and depth that standard butters lack. This elevated fat percentage results in a creamier texture and a more pronounced, cultured flavor, enhancing the overall profile of your baked goods.

Full-Fat Dairy: Full-fat dairy, such as milk, heavy whipping cream, sour cream, and cheese, introduces a luxurious mouthfeel and enhances the flavor complexity of bread. The higher fat content contributes to tenderness and moisture, ensuring your breads are decadent without being greasy.

Sugar: Sugar's role in baking extends beyond mere sweetness; it imparts moisture, fosters caramelization, and bestows a golden hue upon breads. Selecting high-quality sugars, such as C&H and Domino, enhances both the flavor and texture of your bread.

Salt: Salt is the unsung hero, elevating and balancing flavors. Choosing the right type of salt is crucial, as different salts have varying grain sizes and salinity levels, affecting the final taste and texture. I use Diamond Crystal Kosher Salt for baking and Maldon Sea Salt for a finishing touch.

Pure Extracts: Essences like vanilla and almond are the invisible threads connecting flavors. Using pure extracts, as opposed to synthetic versions, imparts authenticity and depth. Neilsen-Massey is an excellent choice.

Fresh Spices: Spices are the storytellers, adding warmth and complexity. Incorporating freshly ground spices ensures that their oils are intact, delivering a potency and vibrancy that the dusty spices hidden in the depths of your pantry cannot match. If your spices are more than a year old, replace them with fresh.

Quality Fruit Spreads: Jams and preserves can add a touch of elegance and depth to your breads, whether baking them into doughs and batters or serving them as an accompaniment. Opting for high-quality fruit spreads made from fresh, whole fruits and minimal sweeteners, such as those from Bonne Maman, provides a wonderful flavor and a pleasing texture that complements many breads.

Essential Equipment

Trusty tools to start your bread-baking off right

Digital scale
Stand mixer
Glass nesting bowls
Liquid-measuring cups
Instant-read thermometer
Parchment paper
13x9-inch baking pan
Baking sheet
Loaf pan
Muffin pan
Wire rack
Whisk
Rubber spatula
Offset spatula
Rolling pin
Ruler
Pastry brush
Pastry blender
Pastry/bench scraper
Unflavored dental floss
Serrated knife

Weigh to Bake

Embrace your digital scale for consistency when baking—it's the secret to precise, reliable, delicious results

MY TOP TIP FOR SUCCESS

Have you ever whipped up a dozen muffins only to have them turn out dry and crumbly or a loaf of sandwich bread that's dense and gummy in the center? The culprit is often inaccurate measurements of ingredients—too little or too much—especially flour. And here's how that happens.

If you were to place a 1-cup measuring cup and a bag of flour in front of five people, ask them to measure 1 cup, and then weigh each person's measurement, you'd end up with different results every time. Why? Because we all have various methods of measuring flour. Some swear by fluffing the flour beforehand. Others dive deep and swoop up, leveling the top of the cup slowly with the back of a butter knife. Some tip the bag with abandon until an avalanche of flour somehow finds its way into the cup, along with a cloud of flour on every surface of their kitchen. This is why a scale carries its weight in gold. When you weigh 125 grams of flour (equivalent to 1 cup by volume) using a scale, it will always be 125 grams. No. Matter. What.

Though all the recipes in this book list both weight (gram) and volume (cup) measures, I strongly encourage measuring by weight. Allow your scale to give you comfort and success in the kitchen by ensuring every ingredient is measured precisely as the recipe intended.

ZWILLING

Dough-cabulary

Get to know these fundamental bread terms

Lean and Enriched Doughs: A lean dough is the most basic type of yeast dough, and only the essentials—flour, water, salt, and yeast—are used to make it. Pizza doughs and French baguettes are classic examples of lean dough. Adding sugar or another sweetener, butter or another fat, milk or another dairy, or eggs to a lean dough makes it enriched. Think buttery brioche, pillowy challah, and melt-in-your-mouth cinnamon rolls.

Hydration: Hydration refers to the ratio of liquid to flour in a yeast dough and is calculated by taking the weight of liquid in a recipe and dividing it by the weight of flour to get a percentage (hydration = liquid weight ÷ flour weight). High-hydration doughs, about 65% or higher, such as ciabatta and focaccia have large air bubbles and an open crumb. Low-hydration doughs, such as bagels and pretzels, typically indicate 50% to 57% hydration.

Shaggy: When a recipe calls for mixing or kneading ingredients together until a "shaggy" dough forms, it should be lumpy or rough (rather than smooth) yet well mixed, without any spots of dry ingredients peeking through.

Windowpane Test: Kneading dough to develop the gluten structure is an essential part of most yeast dough recipes. But how do you know when you've kneaded enough? Enter the windowpane test: Pinch or cut—but don't tear, because this damages the gluten strands—a small, golf ball-size piece of dough. Then gently and slowly pull and rotate the dough out from its center. If the dough is properly kneaded, you will be able to stretch it—without it tearing—until it's thin and translucent. If it tears or breaks during the stretch, give your dough another minute of kneading and then test again. If the dough is too hard to stretch, it's been overmixed; if this happens, stop kneading and move on the next step of the recipe.

Proofing: All yeast bread recipes need time for respiration, which is the process by which yeast can devour sugar and release carbon dioxide, also known as proofing. Yeast dies at temperatures above 130°F (54°C) and goes dormant at 40°F (4°C). For proofing dough, its ideal temperature is a balmy 75°F (24°C) to 80°F (27°C), somewhere draft-free.

Too warm an environment and your dough will overproof; too cold and your dough will struggle to proof at all. Depending on the temperatures and conditions, your dough can rise for 1 to 2 hours. If the room is on the cooler side, it'll take a longer time to proof. Conversely, a hotter room equals a quicker proof. So, how do you know when your dough has properly proofed? Enter the finger dent test.

Finger Dent Test: After your dough has rested for 40 minutes to 1 hour, gently press the pad of your finger about ½ inch into the surface. If your dough has properly proofed, you should be able to watch the dough spring back slightly but still show an indentation. Additionally, the dough will have roughly doubled in size from its original amount. This is perfectly proofed dough.

In underproofed dough, your finger dent will immediately spring back; the gluten is strong, but the carbon dioxide bubbles haven't expanded enough to allow the dough to rise to its full potential. This will produce pale, shrunken bread with less flavor.

In overproofed dough, the finger dent never fills back in but stays firmly there like a stubborn dimple; the carbon dioxide bubbles have stretched the gluten past its limits and popped like burst balloons. Baked overproofed bread can deflate and produce a dense crumb, lacking proper gluten development.

Even if you overmix or overproof your dough, go ahead with your recipe and bake it. The finished product will still be edible, and you don't want to throw away your time and money spent on ingredients. Consider it a learning opportunity for your next bake to be a success.

Doubled in Size: Countless recipes instruct for the dough to rest until it's "doubled in size." The best way to gauge this growth spurt is to use a clear container with measurement markings; my favorite is a glass 8-cup liquid-measuring cup. Once you add the dough, you can see exactly how much your dough expands by the marks on the side.

< FINGER DENT TEST

UNDERPROOFED PERFECTLY PROOFED OVERPROOFED

YEASTED CLASSICS

Get acquainted with this selection of essential breads from a variety of cultures, including Italian focaccia, French baguette, Japanese milk bread, and more

Dutch Oven Bread

Makes 1 loaf

A classic no-knead bread recipe should be as easy as it sounds, with quality ingredients, time, and a Dutch oven doing all the work. This amazing recipe is no exception. Made with an earthy combination of bread flour and whole wheat flour, this dough spends most of its time in the refrigerator, slowly fermenting and building flavor. It bakes in a piping hot Dutch oven, creating a crisp crust and chewy crumb that rivals the best boules from a bakery.

3½ cups (445 grams) bread flour
1¼ cups (156 grams) whole wheat flour
4 teaspoons (12 grams) kosher salt
2¼ teaspoons (7 grams) instant yeast
2 cups (480 grams) warm water (105°F/41°C to 110°F/43°C)
Semolina flour, for dusting

1. In the bowl of a stand mixer, whisk together bread flour, whole wheat flour, salt, and yeast by hand. (Add mix-ins, if using; see page 24.) Add 2 cups (480 grams) warm water; using the paddle attachment, beat at low speed until a sticky dough forms, about 30 seconds.
2. Lightly spray a large bowl with cooking spray. Place dough in bowl. Cover and let rise in a warm, draft-free place (75°/24°C) until doubled in size, 1½ to 2 hours. Refrigerate for at least 2 hours or preferably overnight.
3. Turn out dough onto a work surface heavily dusted with bread flour. Using floured hands, lightly press dough into a 1-inch-thick oval. Grab bottom edge, and gently stretch and fold bottom third over center third. Stretch right side out, and fold right third over center third; repeat with left side. Finish by folding top third over previous folds. Roll loaf away from you seam side down, and using both hands, cup dough and pull it toward you to seal. Rotate dough 90 degrees, and pull again until a tight, smooth boule forms. Place, seam side up, in a banneton (proofing basket) or a medium bowl lined with a kitchen towel heavily dusted with bread flour. Loosely cover dough with towel, and let rise in a warm, draft-free place (75°F/24°C) until puffed, 1 to 1½ hours.
4. When dough has 30 minutes left to rise, place Dutch oven and lid in cold oven. Preheat oven to 500°F (260°C).
5. Dust a piece of parchment paper with semolina flour, and turn out dough, seam side down, onto parchment. (Add toppings, if using; see page 25.) Score dough, if desired.
6. Carefully remove hot Dutch oven from oven; remove lid, and place dough, on parchment, in Dutch oven. Cover with lid, and return to oven. Immediately reduce oven temperature to 425°F (220°C).
7. Bake for 25 minutes. Remove lid, and bake until an instant-read thermometer inserted in center registers 200°F (93°C), 20 to 30 minutes more. Immediately remove loaf from Dutch oven, and let cool completely on a wire rack before slicing. Store in an airtight container for up to 3 days.

Dutch Oven Bread 101

The Best Pot for the Job

Baking bread in a Dutch oven creates a high-heat environment that quickly kills the yeast and forces the bread to rapidly release its gases into an intense wave of steam, a process known as oven spring. Industrial ovens used in professional bakeries do this naturally, but at home, we need help from the Dutch oven lid to trap the steam in with the bread, hydrating the dough, effectively conducting heat, and helping it gain extra height. The steam also interacts with the starches on the bread's surface, creating a crust with a subtle gloss. It leads to an epically crusted and crumbed loaf every time.

You have two main choices of Dutch oven: enamel-coated cast-iron or well-seasoned traditional cast-iron. The difference is in the coating, but the results will remain the same. Be sure the lid fits snugly and securely.

Look for a 6-quart Dutch oven; anything much smaller will keep the bread from rising properly and the crust from forming.

How to Fold

Grab bottom edge, and gently stretch and fold bottom third over center third. Stretch right side out, and fold right third over center third; repeat with left side. Finish by folding top third over previous folds.

Roll loaf away from you seam side down, and using both hands, cup dough and pull it toward you to seal.

Rotate dough 90 degrees, and pull again until a tight, smooth boule forms.

How to Score

When you score, or slice, your dough, you're creating a "weak spot," making sure the gases that rapidly release during oven spring will push in a chosen direction instead of producing an irregularly bubbled top. It's not crucial, but it makes for a lovely loaf.

You'll need an exquisitely sharp blade, like a knife, razor blade, or lame (pronounced "lahm"). I prefer the lame because you can replace the disposable blade as it dulls, and the handle gives you the best ease of movement and feels like an artist's stylus.

Hold your blade at a 45-degree angle and use a light but confident touch to make shallow (¼- to ½-inch-deep) cuts, as too much pressure will pop the air bubbles within.

Start with a basic scoring pattern to get familiar with the movements. A simple arched slash on the side creates a lunar-lip shape, or as the French refer to it, *la grigne*, "the grin" of the loaf. Also popular is the three-slash pattern, where three distinct slices are made across the middle of the loaf.

Bake-It-Your-Own Dutch Oven Bread

Mix and match your favorite flavors to create your perfect version

Mix-In	Prep	Amount	Suggestions	Pro Tip
VEGETABLES	Chop into ¼-inch pieces. (If using peppers, stem and seed them.) Cook over medium heat in 1 tablespoon (14 grams) butter or oil for 8 to 10 minutes to remove excess moisture and temper flavor. Sautéing the vegetables is recommended but not absolutely necessary, but if you decide not to sauté, you'll need to reduce the amount. (See Amount.)	¾ cup (about 203 grams) sautéed vegetables or ½ cup (about 75 grams) diced raw vegetables	Jalapeño, onion, shallot, green onion, bell pepper, garlic Exceptions: Jalapeño is not recommended for sautéing, as it dulls its natural flavor. For garlic, we recommend using 1 small head of roasted garlic.	To roast garlic: Preheat oven to 350°F (180°C). Cut ¼ inch off top end of 1 small head of garlic, keeping cloves intact. Place garlic, cut side up, on foil. Drizzle with 1 teaspoon olive oil, and sprinkle with ¼ teaspoon kosher salt; wrap garlic in foil. Bake until soft, about 1 hour. Let cool completely. Squeeze pulp into a small bowl.
CHEESE	Shred block or wedge cheese or cut into ½-inch cubes.	7- to 8-ounce block or wedge (all shredded, all cubed, or mix half shredded and half cubed) (198 to 226 grams)	Gruyère, Cheddar, Parmesan, fontina, Gouda, Monterey Jack, Havarti	It's best to buy a piece of cheese and shred it, as preshredded cheese is often coated in potato starch and natamycin (an antimold agent). These compounds can affect the way the cheese is distributed and melts in your loaf.
JARRED CONDIMENTS	Drain, rinse, and pat dry if packed in oily brine. Drain and pat dry if packed in water. Roughly chop if large.	1½ cups (202 grams)	Pickled or candied jalapeños, roasted red peppers, pimientos, olives, peperoncini, banana peppers, sun-dried tomatoes	Make sure to rinse condiments packed in oil. The excess oil will affect the flavor and texture of your loaf.
SPICES	Use ground spices, not whole.	2 teaspoons (4 grams) to 1 tablespoon (6 grams) Exception: For everything bagel seasoning, use 2 tablespoons (16 grams)	Black pepper, red pepper (crushed or ground), cinnamon, ginger, cloves, nutmeg, allspice, everything bagel seasoning, garlic powder, onion powder	Keep in mind that many brands of everything bagel seasoning come with salt added, so adjust the salt content of the dough accordingly.

Mix-In	Prep	Amount	Suggestions	Pro Tip
FRESH HERBS	Roughly chop your herbs.	**Mixed Herbs:** ⅓ cup (16 grams), about 1 tablespoon plus 2 teaspoons (4 grams) strong herbs and ¼ cup (12 grams) mild herbs **Strong Herbs:** 2½ tablespoons (8 grams) **Mild Herbs:** ½ cup (24 grams)	**Strong Herbs:** thyme, rosemary, dill, tarragon **Mild Herbs:** basil, cilantro, parsley, chives	Remember to wash and pat dry your fresh herbs before chopping.
DRIED HERBS	Use dried leaves, not ground herbs.	**Strong Herbs:** 2 teaspoons (4 grams) **Mild Herbs:** 2 tablespoons (12 grams)	**Strong Herbs:** oregano, sage, rosemary, herbes de Provence **Mild Herbs:** basil, parsley	Just like spices, dried herbs lose their pungency over time, so check that your herbs haven't exceeded their expiration date. Replace any that are more than a year old.
SEEDS	Soak seeds in 1 cup (240 grams) very hot water (160°F/71°C) for 30 minutes. Drain before using.	½ cup (64 grams) before soaking	Sesame (black or white), poppy, flax, pumpkin, caraway, sunflower, fennel, cumin	Seeds absorb a lot of water, so after soaking, they will be more than 40 grams heavier and increase in size. Soaking the seeds keeps them from absorbing moisture from the bread.
NUTS	Roughly chop and soak raw nuts in 1 cup (240 grams) very hot water (160°F/71°C) for 30 minutes. Drain before using.	1½ cups (170 grams) before soaking	Pecans, walnuts, almonds, pistachios	Like seeds, nuts also absorb a lot of liquid, so they will be heavier and larger after soaking. Soaking nuts keeps them from absorbing moisture from the bread.
DRIED FRUIT	Chop if large. Soak in 1 cup (240 grams) very hot water (160°F/71°C) for 30 minutes. Drain before using.	1½ cups (192 grams) before soaking	Cherries, dates, cranberries, figs, apricots, candied orange peel	Dried fruit will plump up once soaked in the hot water, giving it a better texture in the final loaf. Soaking keeps the dried fruit from taking excess moisture from the bread.
TOPPINGS	Brush loaf with water before sprinkling on toppings.	1 tablespoon (8 grams)	Oats (old-fashioned or steel-cut), millet, nuts, seeds	Score your bread loaf after you've added your toppings so they don't fall into the cuts.

Pane Siciliano

Makes 2 loaves

Pane Siciliano, meaning literally "Sicilian bread," is perfect for accompanying meals or enjoyed on its own with a drizzle of olive oil. Traditionally rolled into an "S" shape called the *occhi* (eyes) *di Santa Lucia,* this gorgeous loaf has a touch of sweetness from honey and is often sprinkled with sesame seeds for added texture and taste.

2 cups (304 grams) semolina flour
1½ cups (191 grams) bread flour
1 tablespoon (9 grams) kosher salt
2¼ teaspoons (7 grams) instant yeast
1¼ cups (300 grams) hot water (120°F/49°C to 130°F/54°C)
2 tablespoons (28 grams) olive oil
1 tablespoon (21 grams) honey
Water, for spraying dough
1 tablespoon (9 grams) sesame seeds

1. In the bowl of a stand mixer, stir together semolina, bread flour, salt, and yeast by hand. Using the paddle attachment, with mixer on low speed, add 1¼ cups (300 grams) hot water, oil, and honey. Beat until a shaggy dough forms; scrape sides of bowl.
2. Switch to the dough hook attachment. Beat at low speed until dough becomes elastic and slightly tacky and pulls away from sides of bowl, 13 to 15 minutes.
3. Lightly oil a large bowl. Place dough in bowl, turning to grease top. Cover and let rise in a warm, draft-free place (75°F/24°C) until doubled in size, 1 to 1½ hours.
4. Line 2 baking sheets with parchment paper.
5. Turn out dough onto a clean surface, and punch down dough. Divide dough in half (about 427 grams each). Roll half of dough into a 24x9-inch rectangle. Starting with one long side, roll up dough into a 24-inch-long log (about 1½ inches thick). Place, seam side down, on a prepared pan. Shape into an "S" shape, rolling each end the opposite way of the other, creating a tight coil at tips of "S" shape. Loosely cover dough with a greased sheet of plastic wrap, and let rise in a warm, draft-free place (75°F/24°C) until puffed, about 1 hour.
6. Roll remaining dough into an 11x9-inch rectangle. Starting with one short side, roll up dough into a log; pinch and tuck ends to seal. Place loaf, seam side down, on remaining prepared pan. Sprinkle semolina on top of dough. Loosely cover and let rise in a warm, draft-free place (75°F/24°C) until puffed, about 1 hour.
7. Preheat oven to 400°F (200°C).
8. Generously spray doughs with water. Sprinkle "S"-shaped dough with semolina; sprinkle sesame seeds onto remaining dough. Score loaves, if desired.
9. Bake until golden brown and an instant-read thermometer inserted in center registers 190°F (88°C), 15 to 20 minutes. Let cool completely on pans on wire racks before slicing or storing. Store in airtight container for up to 3 days.

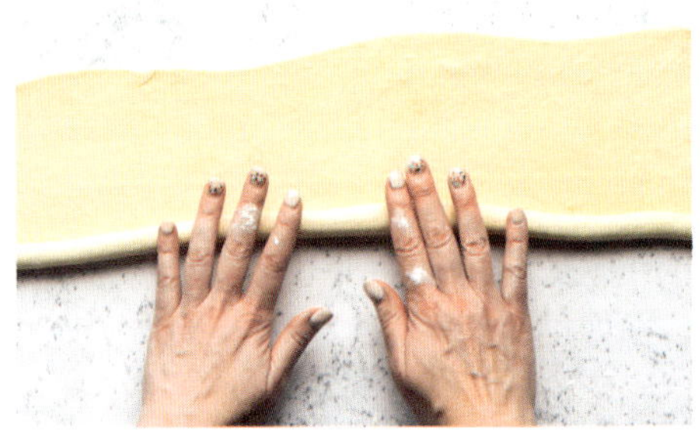

Baguettes

Makes 2 loaves

In France, there are two main varieties of baguette: the *tradition*, which is crafted by hand and uses a lengthy fermentation process, and the *ordinaire*, which can be mechanically produced and may contain additives. As the baguette is a national treasure, the ingredients for a *tradition* are legally regulated in France by Le Decret Pain (The Bread Decree) to only flour, leaven, water, and salt—nothing else—which is exactly how this recipe is formulated.

1½ cups (360 grams) warm water (110°F/43°C to 115°F/46°C), divided
2¼ teaspoons (7 grams) instant yeast
4 cups (508 grams) bread flour, divided
1 tablespoon (9 grams) kosher salt
Semolina flour, for dusting
6 cups (750 grams) ice cubes

1. In the bowl of a stand mixer, whisk together ¾ cup (180 grams) warm water and yeast by hand until dissolved. Add 1⅓ cups (169 grams) bread flour; using the paddle attachment, beat at low speed until combined, about 30 seconds. Cover and let rise in a warm, draft-free place (75°F/24°C) until doubled in size, 30 to 45 minutes.
2. Add salt, remaining 2⅔ cups (339 grams) bread flour, and remaining ¾ cup (180 grams) warm water to yeast mixture, and beat at low speed until dough comes together, about 30 seconds. Switch to the dough hook attachment. Beat at low speed for 2 minutes. (Dough will appear rough rather than smooth at this point.)
3. Spray a large bowl with cooking spray. Place dough in bowl, turning to grease top. Cover and let stand in a warm, draft-free place (75°F/24°C) until smooth and elastic, about 1½ hours, turning every 30 minutes. (To complete a turn, grab underside of dough, stretch it up, and fold it to center of dough. Do this four times around bowl.)
4. Turn out dough onto a work surface very lightly dusted with bread flour, and divide in half. Gently press half of dough into a 9x4-inch rectangle; fold one short side over center third. Fold remaining third over folded portion. Turn dough over so it is seam side down. Repeat with remaining dough. Cover and let stand in a warm, draft-free place (75°F/24°C) for 20 minutes.
5. Line a rimmed baking sheet with parchment paper, letting excess extend over sides of pan. Dust with semolina flour.
6. Gently press each baguette into an 8x6-inch rectangle, with one long side closest to you. Fold top third of dough over center third, pressing to seal. Fold bottom third over folded portion, pressing to seal. Fold dough in half lengthwise so long edges meet. Using the heel of your hand, firmly press edges to seal. Roll into a 15- to 16-inch log of even thickness, pinching ends slightly to taper.
7. Place 1 log, seam side down, on prepared pan, nestling it against one long side of pan. Pull up and fold parchment to create a wall on opposite side of log. Nestle remaining log, seam side down, on other side of parchment wall. Repeat pulling and folding process with parchment to form a wall on opposite side of second log, and weigh down with a kitchen towel to prevent parchment from sliding. Dust tops with flour. Cover and let rise in a warm, draft-free place (75°F/24°C) until slightly puffed, about 45 minutes. (Alternatively, cover and refrigerate for 8 hours or up to overnight. Let rise in a warm, draft-free place [75°F/24°C] until slightly puffed, 30 to 45 minutes.)
8. Place a large cast-iron skillet on bottom rack of oven and a rimmed baking sheet on center rack. Preheat oven to 475°F (250°C). Let skillet heat for 30 to 45 minutes before baking.
9. Remove kitchen towel from pan, and pull parchment flat to separate baguettes. Cut off excess parchment, if desired. Using a lame or sharp paring knife, score top of dough with long diagonal cuts.
10. Place baguettes in oven. Carefully pour ice into preheated skillet. (This will create a lot of steam, so wear oven mitts.) Immediately close oven door.
11. Bake until deep golden brown and an instant-read thermometer inserted in center registers 205°F (96°C) to 210°F (99°C), 13 to 15 minutes. Let cool completely on pan on a wire rack.

Baguettes 101

Turn to Knead

Because this is essentially a no-knead dough, the dough will appear shaggy or rough rather than smooth at the start. A process of folding the dough, called a turn, activates gluten, causing the dough to become smooth and elastic.

To complete one turn, grab the right underside of dough, stretch it up, and fold it to the center of the dough. Move to the left side of the bowl and repeat, grabbing the underside of the dough, gently stretching it to the sky, and then folding the dough over itself. Repeat as before with the top side of the dough. Finish the folding with the bottom side of the dough. The process is repeated a total of three times, once at 30 minutes, again at 1 hour, and the third and final turn will be at 1 hour and 30 minutes. It's helpful to write your turns down at each interval to avoid losing track.

Shaping and Baking

After activating the gluten and proofing the dough, it's time to shape the baguettes. This is a two-part process in which the dough gets a letter fold, a rest, and then a final letter fold before it's shaped into a long, tapered baton.

Fold one short side over center third. Fold remaining third over folded portion. Turn dough over so it is short side down. Repeat with remaining dough. Fold dough in half lengthwise so long edges meet.

Using the heel of your hand, firmly press edges to seal. This helps create a tight loaf that maintains its shape after the final proof. Roll into a 15- to 16-inch log of even thickness, pinching ends slightly to taper.

Place 1 log, seam side down, on prepared pan, nestling it against one long side of pan. Pull up and fold parchment to create a wall on opposite side of log. By nudging the dough against the rim of the baking sheet and using the loaves to hold each other in place, you get the same effect as a proofing cloth, or *couche*, without the specialty equipment.

Nestle remaining log, seam side down, on other side of parchment wall. Repeat pulling and folding process with parchment to form a wall on opposite side of second log, and weigh down with a kitchen towel to prevent parchment from sliding.

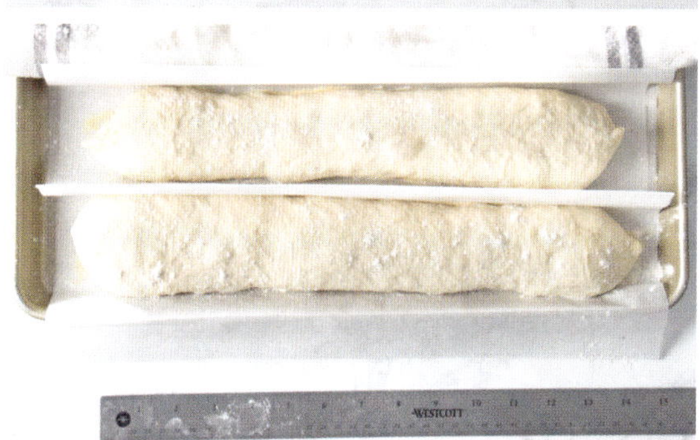

Because the baguettes are baked directly on parchment on the baking sheet, the need to juggle the dough from a cloth to a baking peel to a hot pizza stone is nonexistent, making the transfer to the oven stress-free.

For slightly more flavorful loaves, you can cover the baguettes after shaping and refrigerate for 8 hours or up to overnight. Then let rise in a warm, draft-free place (75°F/24°C) until slightly puffed, 30 to 45 minutes, before baking as directed.

Baguettes traditionally have three to five cuts, which create "ears," or the signature portion of raised crust that develops as bread rises during baking. When you score, or slice, the dough, it creates weak spots, making sure that the gases that rapidly release during oven spring will push in a chosen area instead of producing an irregularly bubbled top.

Using a lame or sharp paring knife, score tops of dough with long diagonal cuts. Confidence is key. Decisive, shallow (¼- to ½-inch-deep) strokes with the blade ensure that the slits in the dough don't appear jagged or irregular. Hold your blade at a 45-degree angle and use a light touch, as too much pressure will drag the dough and pop the air bubbles within.

Don't Skip the Steam

Steam is the crucial step in this recipe that takes the bread from a lackluster loaf to a brilliant baguette. As daunting as it may seem to create steam in your home oven, simply preheating a large cast-iron skillet on the bottom rack of your oven for 30 to 45 minutes before baking is key. After you place the loaves in the oven, grab your bowl of ice and, while wearing oven mitts, carefully add the ice to the cast-iron skillet, creating steam on demand. Move quickly and carefully to minimize heat and steam escaping the oven.

French Bread

Makes 2 (16-inch) loaves

Bring a French boulangerie to your kitchen with this classic bread. The gentle crunch of the crust and soft crumb make these loaves perfect for a *jambon-beurre* (ham and butter) sandwich, a Parisian bistro standard.

2 cups (480 grams) warm water (105°F/41°C to 110°F/43°C), divided
2¼ teaspoons (7 grams) instant yeast
2 teaspoons (8 grams) granulated sugar
5¼ cups (656 grams) all-purpose flour
2 tablespoons (28 grams) unsalted butter, softened
3½ teaspoons (11 grams) kosher salt

1. In a small bowl, whisk together ½ cup (120 grams) warm water, yeast, and sugar. Let stand until foamy, about 5 minutes.
2. In the bowl of a stand mixer fitted with the paddle attachment, beat yeast mixture, flour, butter, salt, and remaining 1½ cups (360 grams) warm water at medium-low speed until combined, 1 to 2 minutes.
3. Switch to the dough hook attachment. Beat at medium-low speed until dough is soft and smooth and pulls away from sides of bowl, 10 to 13 minutes. (Dough will still be very soft.)
4. Spray a large bowl with cooking spray. Place dough in bowl, turning to grease top. Cover with plastic wrap, and let rise in a warm, draft-free place (75°F/24°C) until doubled in size, about 1 hour.
5. Line a large rimmed baking sheet with parchment paper.
6. Turn out dough onto a heavily floured surface, and divide in half. Flatten half of dough into a 13x5-inch rectangle, completely pressing out any air, with one long side closest to you. Starting with long side closest to you, roll up dough into a tight log, tightly pressing seams as you roll. Pinch exterior seam to seal. Place dough log, seam side down, on prepared pan. Repeat with remaining dough. Lightly dust dough logs with flour. Cover with plastic wrap, and let rise in a warm, draft-free place (75°F/24°C) until puffed, about 1 hour.
7. Preheat oven to 425°F (220°C).
8. Using a sharp knife or lame, score each dough log with three diagonal slits.
9. Bake until golden brown and an instant-read thermometer inserted in center registers at least 190°F (88°C), about 20 minutes. Let cool on pan for 10 minutes. Remove from pan, and let cool completely on a wire rack. Store in an airtight container for up to 5 days.

PRO TIPS: Roll the dough in small increments, pressing seams and flattening as you go. This creates a tight log that holds its shape during baking.

This recipe makes two loaves, perfect for gifting a loaf or using leftovers for bread crumbs, croutons, or topping French onion soup. To freeze a loaf, cut in half crosswise, wrap pieces tightly in foil, and store in a plastic freezer bag to prevent off flavors and freezer burn for up to 3 months. Reheat bread in the oven for optimal flavor and texture.

Brioche Loaf

Makes 1 (8½x4½-inch) loaf

This egg- and butter-rich dough is all about ingredient temperatures, allowing for proper gluten development, and ample rise time. Enriched breads notoriously take longer to proof, so patience is key. With braided breads, it's important that the ends are sealed and not tucked or folded under the loaf; it may rise and bake slightly misshapen.

⅓ cup (80 grams) warm whole milk (110°F/43°C to 115°F/46°C)
2¼ teaspoons (7 grams) instant yeast
3 tablespoons (36 grams) granulated sugar, divided
2⅓ to 2⅔ cups (292 to 334 grams) all-purpose flour, divided
2 teaspoons (6 grams) kosher salt
2 large eggs (100 grams), lightly beaten and room temperature
½ cup (113 grams) unsalted butter, cubed and room temperature
1 large egg (50 grams)
1 tablespoon (15 grams) water

1. In a small bowl, stir together warm milk, yeast, and 1 teaspoon (4 grams) sugar. Let stand until foamy, about 5 minutes.
2. In the bowl of a stand mixer, whisk together 1⅓ cups (167 grams) flour, salt, and remaining 2 tablespoons plus 2 teaspoons (32 grams) sugar. Add yeast mixture and beaten eggs. Using the paddle attachment, beat at low speed until combined, about 1 minute. With mixer on low speed, gradually add 1 cup (125 grams) flour, beating until a shaggy dough forms; scrape sides of bowl.
3. Switch to the dough hook attachment. Beat at medium-low speed until dough is smooth, elastic, and slightly tacky, 4 to 6 minutes; add up to remaining ⅓ cup (42 grams) flour, 1 tablespoon (8 grams) at a time, if dough is too sticky. With mixer on medium-low speed, add butter, 1 tablespoon (14 grams) at a time, beating until combined after each addition (6 to 7 minutes total). Beat at medium speed until a smooth, elastic dough forms, 10 to 12 minutes. Turn out onto a lightly floured surface; knead 5 to 8 times, and shape into a smooth round.
4. Lightly oil a large bowl. Place dough in bowl, turning to grease top. Cover and let rise in a warm, draft-free place (75°F/24°C) until doubled in size, 45 minutes to 1 hour.
5. Line a baking sheet with parchment paper.
6. Turn out dough onto a lightly floured surface, and lightly punch down dough. Flatten dough into an 8x6-inch rectangle, and transfer to prepared pan. Cover with plastic wrap, and refrigerate for at least 8 hours or up to overnight.
7. Lightly spray an 8½x4½-inch loaf pan with baking spray with flour. Line pan with parchment paper, letting excess extend over sides of pan.
8. Turn out dough onto a lightly floured surface, and divide into 3 portions (about 217 grams each). Roll each portion into a rope about 14 inches long. Pinch ropes together at one end, and carefully braid together tightly. Pinch ends to seal. Place braid in prepared pan, compressing to fit as needed. (Try not to fold the dough too much under itself; this will result in an irregular bumpy top.) Cover and let rise in a warm, draft-free place (75°F/24°C) until puffed and dough passes the finger dent test (see page 17), 50 to 55 minutes.
9. Preheat oven to 350°F (180°C).
10. In another small bowl, whisk together egg and 1 tablespoon (15 grams) water. Lightly brush egg wash over surface of dough.
11. Bake until golden brown and an instant-read thermometer inserted in center registers 190°F (88°C), 40 to 45 minutes, covering with foil during final 15 minutes of baking to prevent excess browning. Let cool in pan for 10 minutes. Remove from pan, and let cool completely on a wire rack. Store in an airtight container for up 3 days.

Challah

Makes 2 braided loaves

This pillowy bread has a rich, soft, supple dough, perfect for braiding. It's redolent with honey, which gives the dough a floral, slightly sweet aroma. Using oil instead of butter keeps the recipe pareve, meaning it's made without meat, dairy, or their derivatives, according to kosher rules. It also gives the challah a wonderful texture and keeps it fresh longer.

¾ cup (180 grams) lukewarm water (85°F/29°C to 90°F/32°C)
2¼ teaspoons (7 grams) active dry yeast
5¼ cups (667 grams) bread flour, divided
2 tablespoons (24 grams) granulated sugar
4 teaspoons (12 grams) kosher salt
⅓ cup (75 grams) vegetable oil
¼ cup (85 grams) honey
3 large eggs (150 grams), room temperature and divided
2 large egg yolks (37 grams), room temperature
1 tablespoon (15 grams) water

1. In the bowl of a stand mixer, whisk together ¾ cup (180 grams) lukewarm water and yeast by hand until dissolved. Add 1¼ cups (159 grams) bread flour; stir until combined. Cover and let rise in a warm, draft-free place (75°F/24°C) until doubled in size, about 30 minutes.
2. Add sugar, salt, and remaining 4 cups (508 grams) bread flour to yeast mixture.
3. In a medium bowl, whisk together oil, honey, 2 eggs (100 grams), and egg yolks. Add oil mixture to flour mixture. Using the dough hook attachment, beat at low speed until a smooth, slightly tacky, elastic dough comes together, 5 to 7 minutes. Turn out onto a clean surface, and shape into a smooth round.
4. Lightly spray a large bowl with cooking spray. Place dough in bowl, turning to grease top. Cover and let rise in a warm, draft-free place (75°F/24°C) until doubled in size, 1½ to 2 hours.
5. Line a baking sheet with parchment paper.
6. Punch down dough, and turn out onto a clean surface. Cover and let stand for 5 minutes. Divide dough into 12 portions (about 98 grams each). Roll each portion into a 16-inch-long rope. Lightly dust ropes with flour. (This will help keep a defined braid by preventing the ropes from baking together.) Cover 6 ropes with plastic wrap.
7. Pinch together one end of remaining 6 ropes so they are connected. Position pinched ropes at top of work surface, and fan out lengths of ropes so there is space between each.
8. From left to right, count each rope's position from 1 through 6. Cross ropes 1 and 6, switching their positions. Move current rope 6 to center to become rope 4. Move rope 2 to become rope 6. Next, move rope 1 to become rope 3. Move rope 5 to become rope 1. Repeat pattern—6 to 4, 2 to 6, 1 to 3, 5 to 1—until you reach the end. Pinch end of ropes to seal completely, and tuck under. Carefully move braid to prepared pan. Repeat pinching and braiding procedure with remaining ropes (see page 38 for visual guide).
9. In a small bowl, whisk together 1 tablespoon (15 grams) water and remaining 1 egg (50 grams). Using a pastry brush, brush egg wash onto braids. Cover braids with greased plastic wrap, and let rise in a warm, draft-free place (75°F/24°C) until puffed and dough holds an indentation when gently pressed, 1½ to 2 hours.
10. Preheat oven to 375°F (190°C).
11. Brush braids with egg wash.
12. Bake until golden brown and an instant-read thermometer inserted in center registers at least 190°F (88°C), 18 to 25 minutes, covering with foil during final 10 minutes of baking to prevent excess browning. Let cool on pan for 10 minutes. Remove from pan, and let cool completely on a wire rack. Store in an airtight container for up to 5 days.

Challah Braiding 101

Before rolling each portion of dough into a rope, preshape the ropes by bundling up and tucking the edges under, creating a tube shape. This will help you create a nice smooth rope.

Roll each portion into a 16-inch-long rope. Lightly dusting the ropes with flour helps keep a defined braid by preventing the ropes from baking together.

Pinch together one end of 6 ropes so they are connected. Position pinched ropes at top of work surface, and fan out lengths of ropes so there is space between each. Once you have one rope made, simply use it as a benchmark for the length for the rest of your ropes.

From left to right, count each rope's position from 1 through 6. Cross ropes 1 and 6, switching their positions.

Move current rope 6 to center to become rope 4. Move rope 2 to become rope 6.

Next, move rope 1 to become rope 3. Move rope 5 to become rope 1.

Repeat the pattern—6 to 4, 2 to 6, 1 to 3, 5 to 1—until you reach the end.

Pinch the end of ropes together to seal completely, and tuck under. Carefully move braid to prepared pan.

If you notice you missed a step during the braiding process, simply unbraid the ropes and start over—flouring the ropes also allows easy unbraiding.

Japanese Milk Bread

Makes 2 (9x5-inch) loaves

Sweet, downy milk bread gets its unparalleled texture from *tangzhong*, a milk and flour mixture that's cooked on the stove until thickened into a creamy paste. It extends the bread's shelf life and locks in moisture without making the bread heavy. The second crucial part of milk bread is its rolled and spiraled shaping method, which gives the loaf its towering height and iconic swirling imprint on the side crust.

Tangzhong:
¾ **cup (180 grams) whole milk**
¼ **cup (32 grams) bread flour**

Dough:
1⅓ **cups (320 grams) warm whole milk (100°F/38°C to 110°F/43°C)**
⅔ **cup (133 grams) granulated sugar**
1½ **tablespoons (14 grams) active dry yeast**
5½ **cups (699 grams) bread flour**
2 **large eggs (100 grams), lightly beaten and room temperature**
2 **teaspoons (6 grams) kosher salt**
6 **tablespoons (84 grams) unsalted butter, room temperature**

1 **large egg (50 grams)**
1 **tablespoon (15 grams) whole milk**

1. For tangzhong: In a small heavy-bottomed saucepan, whisk together milk and flour. Cook over medium-low heat, whisking constantly, until thickened, an instant-read thermometer registers 149°F (65°C), and whisk leaves lines on bottom of pan. Transfer to a small bowl, and let cool to room temperature before using.
2. For dough: In the bowl of a stand mixer, whisk together warm milk, sugar, and yeast by hand. Let stand until foamy, about 10 minutes.
3. Add tangzhong, flour, beaten eggs, and salt to yeast mixture; stir with a wooden spoon until combined. Using the dough hook attachment, beat at low speed for 5 minutes. Add butter, and beat at medium-low speed for 6 minutes. Scrape sides of bowl, and turn dough over. Beat for 2 minutes. Check dough's gluten development by using the windowpane test. (See page 16.) Cover and let rise in a warm, draft-free place (75°F/24°C) until doubled in size, about 1 hour. Test dough for fermentation by using the finger dent test. (See page 17.)
4. Spray 2 (9x5-inch) loaf pans with cooking spray.
5. Divide dough into 6 portions (252 grams each). Shape each portion into a ball. Roll each ball into a 12x5-inch oval. Fold right third (lengthwise) over center third. Fold left side over center. Using a rolling pin, flatten dough, and reroll into a 12x5-inch oval. Starting with one short side, roll up dough into a log. Place, seam side down, in prepared pan. Repeat with remaining dough, placing 3 portions in each prepared pan. Cover and let rise in a warm, draft-free place (75°F/24°C) until doubled in size, about 1 hour.
6. Preheat oven to 350°F (180°C).
7. In another small bowl, whisk together egg and milk; brush onto dough.
8. Bake until an instant-read thermometer inserted in center registers 190°F (88°C), about 30 minutes, covering with foil during final 10 minutes of baking to prevent excess browning. Immediately remove from pans, and let cool completely on a wire rack. Store in an airtight container for up to 5 days.

PRO TIP: For a decadent treat, cook slices of milk bread in a buttered skillet until golden brown on both sides and then drizzle with sweetened condensed milk. In Japan, condensed milk is used more as a condiment than a baking ingredient. They top shaved ice with it, dip fresh strawberries in it, and, my favorite, spread it on milk bread.

Milk Bread Dough 101

The Tangzhong: This crucial ingredient is what separates milk bread from all other loaves. To make tangzhong, you'll need a small heavy-bottomed saucepan, a proper whisk, steady heat, and undivided attention. Keep your instant-read thermometer on hand, because once the milk and flour begin to congeal, things move quickly. If the tangzhong gets overcooked, it'll become too thick and cross over into genuine roux territory.

Divide dough into 6 portions, weighing each on a scale to ensure even distribution. Roll the dough gently into balls, making sure not to overwork the dough.

Using a rolling pin, flatten each dough ball into a 12x5-inch oval. (These dimensions will help make sure the dough will perfectly fit your pan.)

Fold the right side of the dough (lengthwise) to meet the center of the dough. Repeat on the left side. Your dough should look like a long, skinny strip with a seam. Once folded, flatten the dough with your rolling pin again to its original 12x5-inch oval shape.

Starting with one short side, roll up dough into a 5-inch-wide log. This coiled shape helps give your bread extraordinary lift.

Place 3 spiraled dough rolls, seam side down, into each loaf pan.

Focaccia

Makes 1 (17¼x12¼-inch) loaf

In Italy, regional variations of focaccia range from sweet and enriched to salty and savory, but one thing is certain: This bread is beloved everywhere. This classic version begins with high-protein bread flour, developing its gluten structure through a simple folding process to build elasticity and create a light and airy crumb. The signature dimples allow olive oil to permeate deep into the dough, producing an unbeatably crisp crust and chewy crumb.

2⅓ cups (560 grams) water, room temperature (70°F/21°C to 75°F/24°C)
7 tablespoons (98 grams) extra-virgin olive oil, divided
6 cups (762 grams) bread flour
5 teaspoons (15 grams) kosher salt
2¼ teaspoons (7 grams) instant yeast
1½ cups assorted toppings (see Note)
2 teaspoons (4 grams) flaked sea salt
Garnish: crushed red pepper, ground black pepper

1. In the bowl of a stand mixer fitted with the paddle attachment, place 2⅓ cups (560 grams) room temperature water and 3 tablespoons (42 grams) oil. Add flour, kosher salt, and yeast. Beat at low speed for 4 minutes. Scrape paddle and sides of bowl. Beat at medium-low speed until dough pulls away from sides of bowl and forms a smooth ball on paddle, 2 to 3 minutes.

2. Oil a large bowl. Place dough in bowl. Cover and let rise in a warm, draft-free place (75°F/24°C) for 1½ hours, folding dough in bowl every 30 minutes. (To fold, use wet or oiled hands to reach under one side of dough; gently stretch up, and fold over center. Repeat three more times around bowl; see Turn to Knead on page 30.)

3. Line bottom of a 17¼x12¼-inch rimmed baking sheet with parchment paper. Brush with 2 tablespoons (28 grams) oil.

4. Turn out dough into prepared pan, and using just your fingertips, gently stretch dough to completely fill pan. (If dough is tight and will not stretch completely, let stand for 5 to 10 minutes and then try again.) Cover and let rise in a warm, draft-free place (75°F/24°C) for 30 minutes.

5. Uncover dough, and dimple with your fingertips, touching pan through dough without tearing dough. Cover and let rise in a warm, draft-free place (75°F/24°C) until dough is level with sides of pan, about 30 minutes.

6. Preheat oven to 450°F (230°C).

7. Drizzle remaining 2 tablespoons (28 grams) oil onto dough. Top with desired toppings, and sprinkle with sea salt.

8. Bake for 15 minutes. Reduce oven temperature to 425°F (220°C), and bake until deep golden brown and an instant-read thermometer inserted in center registers 205°F (96°C), about 10 minutes more. Let cool in pan for 10 minutes. Garnish with red pepper and black pepper, if desired. Remove from pan. Serve warm, or let cool completely on a wire rack.

Note: *I love my kitchen scale, but there are so many wonderful toppings to choose from, and their weight will inevitably vary. Instead, measure by volume rather than weight. Mix and match your favorite toppings from page 47.*

Focaccia 101

Turn out dough into prepared pan, and using just your fingertips, gently stretch dough to completely fill pan. If the dough is pulling back and resists stretching completely to the sides, the gluten network may need a brief rest. Let the dough stand for 5 to 10 minutes and then try again.

Cover and let rise in a warm, draft-free place (75°F/24°C) for 30 minutes. During this step, the yeast is releasing carbon dioxide, allowing the dough to rise while building flavor. This dough will be baked in a very hot oven in order to get the proper oven spring and the characteristic golden-brown and crispy exterior.

Uncover dough, and dimple with your fingertips, touching pan through dough without tearing dough. Dimpling the dough creates more surface area, ensuring an even bake and allowing the delicious olive oil to permeate the crust. With your fingers spaced well apart, press into the dough to create a craggy, dimpled appearance.

Cover and let rise in a warm, draft-free place (75°F/24°C) until dough is level with sides of pan, about 30 minutes. During the rise, preheat your oven to 450°F (230°C) to ensure that the oven is the perfect temperature when your dough is ready.

Drizzle remaining 2 tablespoons (28 grams) oil onto dough, and add toppings as desired. The olive oil not only adds flavor and crunch to the crust but it also waterproofs the dough before the toppings are added. From cheeses and cured meats to fragrant fresh herbs, this bread is your blank canvas. Just make sure to limit the amount of excess moisture for best results (i.e., drain wet toppings like olives and artichoke hearts before using).

Unlike other breads that require you to wait until completely cooled before cutting, focaccia can be enjoyed warm. The generous amount of olive oil in the dough helps resist starch retrogradation, and the thin shape allows for moisture to regulate evenly. This bread is also a great candidate for freezing. Cut into pieces, and freeze in an airtight container. Reheat in the oven until just warm for best results.

Topping	Prep	Suggestions	Pro Tips
JARRED CONDIMENTS	Drain if packed in oily brine or water. Roughly chop if large.	Olives, artichoke hearts, capers, roasted red peppers, sun-dried tomatoes	There is no need to rinse oil from oil-packed condiments, but be sure to drain condiments thoroughly before using.
CHEESE	Shred block or wedge cheese. Crumble soft cheeses like goat cheese and feta.	Parmesan, Asiago, fontina, mozzarella, feta, goat cheese	It's best to buy a piece of cheese and shred it, as preshredded cheese is often coated in potato starch and natamycin (an antimold agent). These compounds can affect the way the cheese is distributed and melts on your loaf.
HERBS	Chop fresh herbs or remove small leaves from stems and use leaves whole. Use dried leaves, not ground herbs.	Rosemary, chives, basil, parsley, thyme, oregano, herbes de Provence	Wash and pat dry your fresh herbs before chopping. And just like spices, dried herbs lose their pungency over time, so check that your herbs haven't exceeded their expiration date. Replace any that are more than a year old.
VEGETABLES	Cut vegetables into rounds or cubes. Halve cherry or grape tomatoes; thinly slice and seed peppers and garden tomatoes.	Summer squash, fresh corn, onion, eggplant, tomatoes, garlic, bell peppers, jalapeños	Toss sliced or diced eggplant generously with salt, and let stand for 10 minutes. Rinse and thoroughly pat dry before using. This reduces the bitterness and moisture content of fresh eggplant.
MEATS	Slice meats like pepperoni and soppressata into rounds or cut into cubes. Tear prosciutto or add cubed prosciutto.	Pepperoni, prosciutto, soppressata, salami	Cured meats add flavor and caramelize in the oven.
GARNISH	Lightly sprinkle seasoning on top.	Everything bagel seasoning, flaked sea salt, crushed red pepper, ground black pepper, flavored olive oil, balsamic vinegar reduction	Be mindful of adding too much salt to your bread by way of salty toppings and garnish.

Yeasted Doughnuts

Makes about 15 doughnuts

Lighter than air and perfectly sweet, these doughnuts are ready to be shaped and finished any way your heart desires. Whether dipped in Vanilla Glaze and bursting with apricot jam or strawberry preserves for a fruit-filled delight, dredged in glistening sugar and filled with hazelnut chocolate spread, or stuffed with luscious Vanilla Pastry Cream and topped with Chocolate Glaze for a Boston cream doughnut, the possibilities are endless!

¾ cup (180 grams) warm water (105°F/41°C to 110°F/43°C)
6 tablespoons (72 grams) granulated sugar, divided
1 tablespoon (9 grams) active dry yeast
6¼ cups (781 grams) all-purpose flour
1 cup (240 grams) whole milk, room temperature
¾ cup (95 grams) bread flour
¾ cup (170 grams) unsalted butter, melted and cooled slightly
3 large eggs (150 grams), room temperature
1½ tablespoons (20 grams) vanilla extract
2¼ teaspoons (7 grams) kosher salt
Vegetable oil, for frying
Fillings: Vanilla Pastry Cream (recipe follows), hazelnut chocolate spread, apricot jam, strawberry preserves
Finishes: Vanilla and Chocolate Glazes (recipes follow), granulated sugar

1. In the bowl of a stand mixer, stir together ¾ cup (180 grams) warm water, 2 tablespoons (24 grams) sugar, and yeast by hand. Let stand until foamy, 5 to 10 minutes.
2. Add 2¼ cups (281 grams) all-purpose flour, milk, bread flour, melted butter, eggs, vanilla, salt, and remaining 4 tablespoons (48 grams) sugar to yeast mixture; using the paddle attachment, beat at low speed just until combined. Increase mixer speed to medium; beat until well combined, about 1 minute. With mixer on low speed, gradually add remaining 4 cups (500 grams) all-purpose flour, beating just until combined and a shaggy dough forms, about 1 minute.
3. Switch to the dough hook attachment. Beat at medium-low speed just until dough pulls away from sides of bowl, 8 to 10 minutes. (Dough will still be quite soft and slightly sticky but should not seem excessively wet.)
4. Spray a large bowl with cooking spray. Place dough in bowl, turning to grease top. Cover and let rise in a warm, draft-free place (75°F/24°C) until doubled in size, about 1 hour.
5. Line a rimmed baking sheet with plastic wrap. Punch down dough; turn out onto prepared pan. Tightly cover with plastic wrap, and refrigerate for at least 1 hour or up to overnight.
6. Spray 3 to 4 baking sheets with cooking spray. Cut 15 (5-inch) squares of parchment paper, and place on prepared pans.
7. Lightly dust work surface with all-purpose flour; turn out dough onto prepared surface, and roll to a ½-inch thickness. For regular doughnuts, cut dough with a 3½-inch doughnut cutter or a 3½-inch round cutter with a 1-inch cutter for the center, dipped in flour. For a filled doughnut, cut dough with just a 3½-inch round cutter dipped in flour. Gently transfer doughnuts to prepared parchment squares, spacing at least 2 inches apart. Transfer doughnut holes to prepared parchment squares.
8. Reroll scraps; let dough stand for 10 minutes. Cut dough, and place on prepared parchment squares. (Discard any remaining dough scraps.) Cover with plastic wrap, and let rise in a warm, draft-free place (75°F/24°C) until puffed, about 45 minutes for doughnut holes and 1 to 1½ hours for doughnuts.
9. In a 4- to 6-quart cast-iron Dutch oven or other heavy-bottomed saucepan, pour oil to a depth of 2 inches, and heat over medium heat until a deep-fry thermometer registers 365°F (185°C). Line several rimmed baking sheets with paper towels.
10. Using parchment paper to pick up doughnut holes, transfer doughnut holes in batches to hot oil, letting holes gently fall off parchment into oil. (See Note.) Fry in batches until golden brown, about 1 minute per side. Using a spider strainer, remove doughnut holes, and let drain on prepared pans.

11. Using parchment paper to pick up doughnuts, transfer doughnuts in batches to hot oil, letting doughnuts gently fall off parchment into oil. (See Note.) Fry doughnuts in batches until golden brown, about 1 minute per side. Using a spider strainer, remove doughnuts, and let drain on prepared pans. Fill and glaze as desired. (See page 51 for more details.) Best served same day.

Note: *If the dough is sticking to the parchment at any point or you find it easier, it is fine to place the parchment in the oil. Once the doughnut starts to fry, it will release and you can use tongs to remove the parchment from the oil.*

Vanilla Pastry Cream

Makes 1⅔ cups

1½ cups (360 grams) whole milk
½ cup (100 grams) granulated sugar, divided
1 teaspoon vanilla extract
4 large egg yolks (74 grams)
3½ tablespoons (28 grams) cornstarch
½ teaspoon kosher salt
2 tablespoons (28 grams) unsalted butter, softened

1. In a large saucepan, whisk together milk, ¼ cup (50 grams) sugar, and vanilla. Heat over medium heat until steaming. (Do not boil.)
2. In a large bowl, whisk together egg yolks, cornstarch, salt, and remaining ¼ cup (50 grams) sugar. Gradually add warm milk mixture, whisking constantly. Pour egg yolk mixture into saucepan, and cook over medium heat, whisking constantly, until thickened and boiling, 4 to 5 minutes.
3. Strain mixture through a fine-mesh sieve into another large bowl. Stir in butter until melted and well combined. Cover with plastic wrap, pressing wrap directly onto surface of pastry cream to prevent a skin from forming. Refrigerate until thick and cold, about 4 hours, or overnight.

Vanilla Glaze

Makes about 2 cups

3½ cups (420 grams) confectioners' sugar, sifted
5 tablespoons (75 grams) whole milk
2½ tablespoons (53 grams) light corn syrup
½ teaspoon kosher salt
½ teaspoon vanilla extract

1. In a medium bowl, whisk together all ingredients until smooth and well combined. Use immediately.

Chocolate Glaze

Makes about 1½ cups

3 cups (360 grams) confectioners' sugar
⅓ cup (25 grams) Dutch process cocoa powder
½ teaspoon kosher salt
6 tablespoons (90 grams) whole milk
1½ tablespoons (32 grams) light corn syrup
1½ teaspoons (6 grams) vanilla extract

1. In a medium bowl, sift together confectioners' sugar, cocoa, and salt. Whisk in milk, corn syrup, and vanilla until smooth and well combined. Use immediately.

Doughnut 101

Let It Rise

If you have time, you can make the dough and let it rest overnight for the second rise. This process is known as cold fermentation, which gives the dough a more complex flavor and lovely texture. However, if you don't have time to make the dough the day before, you can still make it with a shorter resting time. Just be sure to complete the one-hour chill time, as the dough will be easier to work with when cold.

Cut and Proof the Dough

When punching out your doughnuts, don't twist the cutter and keep it well-floured between each cut so it doesn't catch on the sticky dough.

After you've rerolled the scraps for a second cutting, let the dough rest for 10 minutes to allow it to relax and make it easier to work with. When gently pressed, properly proofed doughnuts will hold the indentation without collapsing. If the dough just bounces back, the doughnuts are still underproofed and need more time. Wait another 5 to 10 minutes and then perform another finger dent test. After the dough has risen and puffed, you can easily freeze yeasted doughnut dough to fry later. Freeze the cut-out dough in a single layer until solid. Place the frozen cut-out dough in a plastic freezer bag. Be sure to let frozen dough fully thaw in a single layer at room temperature before frying.

A Feel for Frying

Before you fry, you need to have your oil prepped and ready. That means having it poured to a depth of 2 inches in your pot and at the temperature called for in the recipe (365°F/185°C in the case of our Yeasted Doughnuts).

Using parchment helps you easily and safely transfer and lower dough into the hot oil. Bubbles should immediately begin forming around the dough; if not, check the oil's temperature to ensure it's hot enough.

While frying, it's important not to overcrowd the pot, or it'll reduce the temperature of the oil. In a minute, you'll turn them to reveal a golden underside. When a yeasted doughnut is fried, it should have a pale ring around its center, known as the "proof line." This happens because air inside the dough makes the doughnut float just above its midpoint. As a result, the top and bottom fry in the oil while a ring around the middle stays just above the oil level. Once the doughnuts have been turned and fried until golden, you'll want to transfer them to the prepared pans to cool immediately.

Time to Fill

Spoon desired fillings into separate pastry bags fitted with a small round piping tip (Ateco #802). We used Vanilla Pastry Cream, hazelnut chocolate spread, apricot jam, and strawberry preserves.

For rounds: Insert a thin, sharp knife into one side of cooled doughnut, about halfway into doughnut. Insert piping tip into cut hole, and fill until doughnut feels heavier and filling begins to come out of the hole. Rings and rounds will hold no more than about 3 tablespoons of filling.

For rings: Using a small paring knife, make 4 small holes in bottom of cooled doughnut. Insert piping tip into each cut hole, and slowly fill until filling begins to come out of the hole.

For doughnut holes: Insert a thin, sharp knife halfway into cooled doughnut hole. Insert piping tip into cut hole, and slowly fill until resistance is met. Doughnut holes will hold no more than 1 to 2 teaspoons of filling.

Tips for Toppings

You have a few options for topping your doughnuts: a dip into a delightful Chocolate or Vanilla Glaze or a roll in sugar for a crunchy exterior. If you opt for a glaze, make sure your doughnut has completely cooled after frying, or it'll melt the glaze. However, a still-warm doughnut is required for the sugar to stick to the surface.

For sugar-coated doughnuts and holes: In a large bowl, place 2 to 3 cups (400 to 600 grams) granulated sugar. Let doughnuts drain and cool just until excess oil has dripped off. Working in batches, gently toss warm doughnuts in granulated sugar to coat. Let cool completely. Fill doughnuts after coating in sugar and letting cool completely, if desired.

For glazed doughnuts and holes: Line rimmed baking sheets with parchment paper; place wire racks on prepared pans. Dip doughnuts, one at a time, halfway into Vanilla Glaze or Chocolate Glaze; lift straight up and then swirl in a circular motion, letting excess drip off. Place doughnuts and holes, glaze side up, on prepared rack. Serve immediately, or let stand until glaze is set, about 20 minutes.

English Muffins

Makes 12 English muffins

Whether dressed simply with butter and jam or topped with Canadian bacon, poached eggs, and hollandaise for the ultimate eggs Benedict, these English muffins are sure to become a new breakfast staple. With the English muffins' crisp, perfectly golden crusts and tender, light centers, other breakfast breads simply can't compete. Just beware: It's best practice to pry the bread apart with a fork in order to preserve the nooks and crannies of your freshly made English muffins. Once toasted, every pocket and peak becomes a vessel for pools of butter, honey, and any other scrumptious topping you can dream up.

---

4 cups (508 grams) bread flour
3¼ teaspoons (10 grams) kosher salt
2¼ teaspoons (7 grams) active dry yeast
1 teaspoon granulated sugar
1¾ cups (420 grams) lukewarm water (85°F/29°C to 90°F/32°C)
1 teaspoon neutral oil
Semolina flour, for dusting

1. In the bowl of a stand mixer, whisk together bread flour, salt, yeast, and sugar by hand. Add 1¾ cups (420 grams) lukewarm water and oil. Using the dough hook attachment, beat at medium-low speed until ingredients come together, 1 to 2 minutes, stopping to scrape sides of bowl. (Mixture will be shaggy, but no dry bits of flour should remain.) Increase mixer speed to medium, and beat until dough is shiny, smooth, and elastic (does not tear when pulled), pulls away from sides of bowl completely, and forms a ball around dough hook, 13 to 15 minutes.
2. Spray a medium bowl with cooking spray. Place dough in bowl. Cover and refrigerate overnight.
3. Line 2 baking sheets with parchment paper. Dust with semolina flour. If using English muffin rings, spray with cooking spray. Place semolina flour on a plate, and coat rings with semolina flour by rotating rings in a quick circular motion on plate.
4. Turn out dough onto a work surface lightly dusted with bread flour, and lightly press with fingertips until even. Divide dough into 12 portions (about 78 grams each). Place on lightly floured surface, and using floured hands, press with your fingertips to an even thickness. Starting at one point on outside edge, pull (or fold) edge toward center, and lightly press to seal. Continue clockwise around edge until you reach original starting point. Turn seam side down, and using your hands, pull dough across lightly floured surface until smooth and round and holds its shape. Repeat with remaining dough, and place at least 3 inches apart on prepared pans. If using, place prepared rings around dough. Sprinkle tops of dough with semolina flour. Loosely cover with plastic wrap, and let rise in a warm, draft-free place (75°F/24°C) until puffed and dough jiggles slightly when pan is moved, about 1 hour. (If not using rings, it is important to spray the plastic wrap with cooking spray before covering.)
5. Preheat electric griddle to 350°F (180°C), or preheat a cast-iron griddle pan to medium heat. (See Note.) Lightly spray griddle with cooking spray. Using 2 greased spatulas, gently move dough (and rings) to preheated surface, placing at least 1½ inches apart. Cook until bottoms are golden brown and tops are puffed and look dry/matte, about 8 minutes for electric griddle or about 5 minutes for cast-iron griddle. Turn English muffins, and remove rings, if using; cook until bottoms are golden brown and an instant-read thermometer inserted in center registers 205°F (96°C) to 210°F (99°C), about 8 minutes for electric griddle or about 5 minutes for cast-iron griddle. If English muffins register below 205°F (96°C), turn back over, and cook until done, 1 to 3 minutes. Place on a wire rack. Wipe griddle surface clean, and spray with cooking spray before cooking next batch. Let English muffins cool completely before splitting with a fork. Serve toasted and warm.

Note: *A cast-iron skillet can be used, but the sides make it harder to turn the English muffins over. A 12-inch skillet would be recommended and only 2 English muffins cooked at a time.*

English Muffins 101

Shape Your Dough: After the overnight rest, your dough will feel soft, elastic, and slightly tacky. Turn it out onto a work surface lightly dusted with bread flour and gently press it to an even thickness—avoid adding too much flour, as this dough relies on higher hydration for its signature nooks and crannies.

Divide into equal portions. Working with one portion at a time, fold the edges toward the center and then turn seam side down and lightly drag against the work surface to create surface tension. This gentle shaping preserves the gas developed during fermentation, ensuring a light, airy interior.

Let Rise in Rings: Sprinkle tops lightly with semolina and cover. Let rise in a warm, draft-free place until noticeably puffed and slightly jiggly—about 1 hour. This final proof allows the dough to relax and expand, setting up the structure needed for even cooking and a well-defined crumb.

Time to Cook: Preheat a griddle pan or griddle to medium heat (about 350°F/180°C). Lightly grease the surface. Using spatulas, gently transfer dough (with rings, if using) to the griddle, spacing evenly.

Cook until the bottoms are golden brown and the tops appear dry and matte, about 5 to 8 minutes depending on your heat source. The dough should visibly puff as steam and fermentation gases expand, helping create those classic interior pockets.

Turn the muffins and remove rings, if using. Continue cooking until the second side is golden brown and an instant-read thermometer registers 205°F (96°C) to 210°F (99°C) in the center.

If the exterior browns too quickly before the interior is done, turn again briefly to finish cooking through.

Transfer to a wire rack and let cool completely before splitting—use a fork, not a knife, to preserve the interior structure and create those signature craggy nooks and crannies.

Bagels

Makes 12 bagels

Any way you finish them, these ringed beauties are the ideal chewy canvas for your choice of toppings.

7 cups (889 grams) bread flour
2 tablespoons (18 grams) kosher salt
1¾ teaspoons (5 grams) instant yeast
2⅓ cups (560 grams) hot water (120°F/49°C to 130°F/54°C)
½ cup (170 grams) plus 2 tablespoons (42 grams) barley malt syrup, divided
8 cups (1,920 grams) plus 1 tablespoon (15 grams) water, divided
1 large egg white (30 grams)
Everything bagel seasoning, sesame seeds, poppy seeds, and freshly grated Asiago cheese, for topping

1. In the bowl of a stand mixer, whisk together flour, salt, and yeast by hand. Add 2⅓ cups (560 grams) hot water and 2 tablespoons (42 grams) barley malt syrup; using the paddle attachment, beat at low speed until a shaggy dough forms, about 1 minute.
2. Switch to the dough hook attachment. Beat at low speed until dough pulls away from sides and bottom of bowl, about 8 minutes. (Dough will be elastic but may not look completely smooth.) Turn out dough onto a lightly floured surface, and shape into a smooth ball.
3. Lightly oil a large bowl. Place dough in bowl, turning to grease top. Cover and let rise in a warm, draft-free place (75°F/24°C) until doubled in size, 45 minutes to 1 hour.
4. Place a large sheet of parchment paper in a warm, draft-free place (75°F/24°C); dust parchment with flour.
5. Divide dough into 12 portions (about 107 grams each). Shape each portion into a ball. Place 1 ball in your hand. Using your thumb and forefinger, pinch a hole in center of ball, and stretch hole to about 3 inches wide. Place on prepared parchment. Repeat with remaining dough balls. (Once dough contracts, the holes should be 1 to 1½ inches wide.) Cover and let rise until puffed, 15 to 30 minutes.
6. Preheat oven to 400°F (200°C). Line baking sheets with parchment paper.
7. In a large stockpot, heat 8 cups (1,920 grams) water and remaining ½ cup (170 grams) barley malt syrup over medium-low heat until barely simmering. (Do not boil.) Carefully drop shaped dough, 1 to 2 at a time, into simmering water-syrup mixture; cook for 10 seconds per side, and immediately transfer to prepared pans.
8. In a small bowl, whisk together egg white and remaining 1 tablespoon (15 grams) water; brush onto dough, and sprinkle with desired toppings. (See Note.)
9. Bake until golden brown, 20 to 25 minutes. Let cool on pans for 10 minutes. Best served warm. Store in an airtight container for up to 3 days.

Note: *Use 1 tablespoon (9 grams) everything bagel seasoning, sesame seeds, or poppy seeds per bagel; use ¼ cup (28 grams) shredded Asiago cheese per bagel.*

Bagels 101

Place dough ball on a lightly floured surface, and cup the top of the dough loosely with your hand. Roll the dough in small circles until it becomes taut, pulling slightly on the surface. If the dough begins to tear, stop—you've gone too far. A tight dough ball is key, because any loose air bubbles will affect the signature crumb of the bagel.

Using your thumb and forefinger, pinch a hole through the center of the dough. Poking through on both sides (rather than poking a hole through with just the thumb) helps break the seal without tearing the dough.

Rotate the dough between your hands, gently squeezing and stretching out the hole to about 3 inches wide, being careful not to tug too hard and overwork the dough. This will feel and look like an exaggerated stretch, but the strong gluten structure in the dough will ensure that it will spring back to a much more conservative 1- to 1½-inch diameter after a few minutes.

Even as you place your stretched-out shaped dough onto the prepared pan, you'll notice it snapping back into a tighter tube. Allow it to puff up for 15 to 30 minutes, loosely covered with plastic wrap. Covering your dough during the rise is key; otherwise, it'll begin to dry out in the open air.

In the old days, this step would be called "kettling," because bakers would boil their shaped bagel dough in large kettles. Boiling is crucial to giving your bagel that signature chew and dense crumb. The hot water causes the dough's starchy surface to gel and form a skin, which will then bake into a glossy, chewy crust.

Of course, "boiling" is an exaggerated term for the process. Instead, you'll bring your pot of water and barley malt syrup to a gentle simmer. Working in batches of 1 or 2, use a slotted spoon or ladle to drop the shaped dough into the water. Simmer for 10 seconds on each side. The longer the boil, the bouncier and more puckered the bagel will be, so know that every extra second in the pot significantly changes the texture and appearance of the bagel.

Tasty Toppings

Asiago is the king of cheeses, nutty and salty, crispy and creamy, all at once. Use ¼ cup (28 grams) grated cheese per bagel, and pile it on.

Everything bagel seasoning is a blend of seeds, garlic, onion, and salt. Use 1 tablespoon (9 grams) per bagel.

Sesame seeds are a standard bagel topper for a reason. Toasted white seeds offer crunch and a slight nuttiness, and when mixed with black seeds, add a visual pop. Use a blended 1 tablespoon (9 grams) of seeds per bagel.

Blue-black poppy seeds are a common ingredient in Jewish baking, so it's unsurprising to find them gracing the top of a bagel. They impart a distinctly earthy flavor and tiny crunch to your bagels. Use 1 tablespoon (9 grams) per bagel.

SANDWICH BREADS and DINNER ROLLS

Whether you're filling a breadbasket for a suppertime side or feeding a crowd with burgers and sandwiches, these recipes are versatile enough to complement any meal

Clover Beer Rolls

Makes 24 rolls

I infused this dough with an amber ale because it offers subtle notes of toasty malt and sweet citrus that balance out the savory cheese and roasted garlic. A hoppy beer (like an IPA) would make the bread too bitter.

Roasted garlic:
1 large head garlic (about 73 grams)
1 teaspoon olive oil
¼ teaspoon kosher salt

Rolls:
1¾ cups plus 2 tablespoons (450 grams) warm amber ale (105°F/41°C to 110°F/43°C), divided
1½ tablespoons (14 grams) active dry yeast
1½ tablespoons (32 grams) honey
5⅔ cups (680 grams) bread flour
10 ounces (283 grams) freshly grated Parmesan cheese, divided
2 tablespoons (24 grams) granulated sugar
2 tablespoons (4 grams) chopped fresh parsley
1 tablespoon (9 grams) kosher salt
¼ cup (57 grams) unsalted butter, melted

Garnish: flaked sea salt, chopped fresh parsley

1. Preheat oven to 350°F (180°C).
2. For roasted garlic: Cut ¼ inch off top end of garlic, keeping cloves intact. Place garlic, cut side up, on foil. Drizzle with oil, and sprinkle with kosher salt; wrap garlic in foil.
3. Bake until soft, about 1 hour. Let cool completely. Squeeze pulp into a small bowl, and mash with a fork.
4. For rolls: In a small bowl, stir together 1 cup (240 grams) warm beer, yeast, and honey. Let stand until foamy, about 5 minutes.
5. In the bowl of a stand mixer fitted with the dough hook attachment, combine flour, 8 ounces (226 grams) cheese, roasted garlic, sugar, parsley, and kosher salt. Add yeast mixture and remaining ¾ cup plus 2 tablespoons (210 grams) warm beer, and beat at low speed until a smooth, elastic dough forms, 8 to 9 minutes.
6. Spray a large bowl with cooking spray. Place dough in bowl, turning to grease top. Cover and let rise in a warm, draft-free place (75°F/24°C) until doubled in size, 30 to 40 minutes.
7. Spray 2 (12-cup) muffin pans with cooking spray.
8. Punch down dough, and turn out onto a lightly floured surface. Divide dough into 24 portions (about 60 grams each). Working with 1 portion at a time (keep remaining dough covered to prevent it from drying out), divide each into 3 pieces (about 20 grams each). Roll each piece into a ball. Place 3 dough balls in each prepared muffin cup. Cover and let rise in a warm, draft-free place (75°F/24°C) until doubled in size, about 40 minutes.
9. Preheat oven to 400°F (200°C).
10. Brush melted butter onto dough, and sprinkle remaining 2 ounces (57 grams) cheese on top.
11. Bake until golden brown and an instant-read thermometer inserted in center registers 190°F (88°C), 8 to 10 minutes, rotating pans halfway through baking. Brush with melted butter again, and garnish with sea salt and parsley, if desired. Best served warm. Store in an airtight container for up to 3 days.

Honey-Wheat Bread

Makes 1 (9x5-inch) loaf

Using a combination of all-purpose and whole wheat flours gives this loaf a tender crumb and a subtle toasty, nutty flavor. With a sweetness that doesn't overwhelm, this versatile bread is a great base for all kinds of sandwiches, whether summer tomato, turkey and Swiss, or classic peanut butter and jelly.

---

1 cup (240 grams) warm water (105°F/41°C to 110°F/43°C)
2 tablespoons (24 grams) granulated sugar
2¼ teaspoons (7 grams) active dry yeast
2 cups (250 grams) whole wheat flour
1½ cups (188 grams) all-purpose flour
3 tablespoons (63 grams) honey
2 large eggs (100 grams), room temperature and divided
1 tablespoon (14 grams) unsalted butter, softened
2 teaspoons (6 grams) kosher salt
1 tablespoon (15 grams) water
Quick-cooking oats, for sprinkling

1. In a small bowl, whisk together 1 cup (240 grams) warm water, sugar, and yeast. Let stand until foamy, about 5 minutes.
2. In the bowl of a stand mixer fitted with the paddle attachment, combine flours, honey, 1 egg (50 grams), butter, and salt. Add yeast mixture, and beat at low speed until combined and a shaggy dough forms.
3. Switch to the dough hook attachment. Beat at medium-low speed until dough pulls away from sides of bowl, 5 to 8 minutes. (Dough will be soft and slightly sticky.)
4. Oil a large bowl. Place dough in bowl, turning to grease top. Cover and let rise in a warm, draft-free place (75°F/24°C) until doubled in size, 45 minutes to 1 hour.
5. Lightly dust work surface with all-purpose flour. Punch down dough, and turn out onto prepared surface. Cover and let stand for 20 minutes. Pat dough into a 9x7-inch rectangle, with one short side closest to you. Fold bottom third of dough over center third; starting at short side where dough is folded, roll up dough into a log. Pull log, seam side down, toward you to create tension on surface.
6. Lightly spray a 9x5-inch loaf pan with baking spray with flour. Place dough, seam side down, in prepared pan, tucking ends slightly. Cover and let rise in a warm, draft-free place (75°F/24°C) until doubled in size and risen just above sides of pan, about 1½ hours.
7. Preheat oven to 375°F (190°C).
8. In another small bowl, whisk together 1 tablespoon (15 grams) water and remaining 1 egg (50 grams). Using a pastry brush, brush egg wash onto dough; sprinkle oats on top.
9. Bake until golden brown and an instant-read thermometer inserted in center registers at least 190°F (88°C), about 30 minutes. Let cool in pan for 15 minutes. Remove from pan, and let cool completely on a wire rack. Store in an airtight container for up to 5 days, or tightly wrap in plastic wrap and freeze for up to 3 months.

Sourdough Sandwich Loaf

Makes 1 (9x5-inch) loaf

You probably envision sourdough bread as a crusty, chewy boule, but this version is a richly flavored, soft-textured loaf. It's the perfect bread for your ultimate grilled cheese, or simply toasted until golden brown and slathered with salted butter.

1½ cups (190 grams) bread flour, plus more for dusting
1½ cups (195 grams) whole wheat flour
2½ teaspoons (8 grams) kosher salt
1¼ cups (300 grams) lukewarm water (80°F/27°C to 90°F/32°C)
½ cup (113 grams) ripe Sourdough Starter (recipe and technique on page 68)
2 tablespoons (28 grams) olive oil

1. In a large bowl, whisk together bread flour, whole wheat flour, and salt. Add 1¼ cups (300 grams) warm water, Sourdough Starter, and oil; stir until a shaggy dough forms and no dry spots remain.
2. Cover and let rise in a warm, draft-free place (75°F/24°C) for 4 hours, folding dough in bowl every 1 hour. (To fold, carefully pull and stretch one side of dough, and fold it over on itself. Repeat for all four sides; see Turn to Knead on page 30.) After final fold, cover and refrigerate dough for at least 8 hours or up to 24 hours.
3. Lightly dust work surface with all-purpose flour. Turn out dough onto prepared surface. Cover and let stand for 20 minutes. Pat dough into a 9x7-inch rectangle, with one short side closest to you. Fold bottom third of dough over center third; starting at short side where dough is folded, roll up dough into a log. Pull log, seam side down, toward you to create tension on surface.
4. Lightly spray a 9x5-inch loaf pan with baking spray with flour. Place dough, seam side down, in prepared pan. Cover and let rise in a warm, draft-free place (75°F/24°C) until doubled in size and risen just above sides of pan, 2½ to 3 hours.
5. Preheat oven to 450°F (230°C).
6. Lightly dust top of dough with bread flour. Place in oven. Immediately reduce oven temperature to 425°F (220°C).
7. Bake until golden brown and an instant-read thermometer inserted in center registers 190°F (88°C), about 30 minutes, covering with foil during final 10 minutes of baking to prevent excess browning. Let cool in pan on a wire rack for 15 minutes. Remove from pan, and let cool completely on a wire rack. Store in an airtight container for up to 1 week, or tightly wrap in plastic wrap and freeze for up to 3 months.

PRO TIP: Olive oil is added to enrich and soften the loaf to create the bounce and texture of sandwich bread.

Sourdough Starter 101

Sourdough is an enigma, as it's both simple and complex. It's a naturally leavened bread that comes from the starter, which is the life force of your bread. A starter is a mixture of flour and water that absorbs the yeast and bacteria from the air and forms a stable colony. The living organisms feed on the flour, producing gas and lactic acid, which both flavor and raise the sourdough.

Don't Toss the Discard: When you remove some of the mature starter, you offer the yeast more food each time you feed it so it's not battling with so many other yeast cells to get enough to eat. But you don't have to toss the discard if you don't want to. Use it for baking like with our Sourdough Discard Banana Bread on page 100, or place the discard in a separate container and keep feeding it. After day 7, the discard will be strong enough to give to a friend.

Day 1: In a clear glass jar or similar container, stir together ¼ cup (32 grams) bread flour, ¼ cup (33 grams) whole wheat flour, and ¼ cup (60 grams) lukewarm water (75°F/24°C to 85°F/29°C). Loosely cover with lid or a small cloth. Let stand at room temperature for 24 hours.

Day 2: You may or may not see much activity during the first 24 hours; regardless, you need to discard about half of the starter. Discard (in a garbage can, as discarding it in the kitchen sink could cause a clog) all but 4 tablespoons (57 grams) flour mixture remaining in jar. Add ½ cup (64 grams) bread flour and ¼ cup (60 grams) lukewarm water (75°F/24°C to 85°F/29°C). (This mixture of flour and water is called the "feed" because it is literally food for the natural yeast and bacteria.) Stir until combined. Loosely cover with lid or a small cloth. Let stand at room temperature for 24 hours.

Days 3 through 6: Continue to discard and feed sourdough following the same procedure and with the same mixture as on day 2. The starter should be showing significant signs of activity. Check on your starter every 6 to 10 hours to see if a routine is building.

Container Clarity

Clear glass, enameled crockery, stainless steel, or food-grade plastic containers all work for a starter—just ensure it's large enough to contain the starter as it grows. Other metals are not recommended for long-term storage. At the beginning of day 3, mark your container with a piece of tape or a rubber band to indicate the post-feeding starter level to make it easy to track how much your starter has risen.

Day 7: Discard and feed your starter as you did on day 2. Check activity level by carefully dropping a small spoonful into a glass of cold water; if it floats, it's active. If it does not float, it needs a little more time to develop. If there has been little activity in your starter at this point, it might need some help. Consider feeding it twice a day (or every 10 to 12 hours) and leaving it in a warmer spot to increase activity.

Days 8 through 13: Continue to feed your starter daily (or twice a day if it needs the help). Monitor its activity level and smell. It should smell slightly sour and yeasty, kind of like ripe cheese or yogurt.

Day 14: Congratulations! You should have a healthy, thriving sourdough starter on your hands. At this point, it should rise and fall on a consistent timeline, smell ripe, and pass the float test from day 7. You should be able to start baking with your starter, and it is ready for cold storage.

Day 15 and beyond: If you are not planning on baking bread regularly, store your starter in the refrigerator after day 14. Feed your starter as you have and let it stand at room temperature just until you begin to see signs of activity, 1 to 2 hours. Cover tightly with a lid and refrigerate; refrigerated starters need to be fed once a week. To use a starter from the refrigerator, let it stand at room temperature until it peaks and shows signs of activity again after 1 to 2 feedings.

Stopping Your Starter for a Spell: You can dry out your healthy, thriving starter by spreading it in a very thin layer on a parchment paper-lined baking sheet and leaving it out until it's brittle. Then break it into pieces, keep the dried starter in an airtight container, and when you want to use it again, rehydrate it by dissolving it in warm water and feeding it as usual.

Fold and Shape

Lightly dust work surface with all-purpose flour. Turn out dough onto prepared surface. Cover and let stand for 20 minutes. Pat dough into a 9x7-inch rectangle, with one short side closest to you. Fold bottom third of dough over center third; starting at short side where dough is folded, roll up dough into a log. Pull log, seam side down, toward you to create tension on surface. Folding and rolling up the dough creates tension, and that tension helps the loaf rise up and out.

Lightly spray a 9x5-inch loaf pan with baking spray with flour. Place dough, seam side down, in prepared pan. Cover and let rise in a warm, draft-free place (75°F/24°C) until doubled in size and risen just above sides of pan, 2½ to 3 hours. After its final rise, you can tell the dough has been proofed by seeing if the dough is relaxed. Test this by pushing your finger into the dough gently. If the indentation springs back slowly, it's ready to bake.

Potato Rolls

Makes 6 rolls

Using mashed potato in the dough creates a tighter crumb structure while also giving the rolls extra moisture and a soft texture. These pillowy rolls absorb all the flavors of your patties and toppings for your ultimate burger.

3¼ to 3½ cups (407 to 438 grams) all-purpose flour, divided
2 tablespoons (24 grams) granulated sugar
2¼ teaspoons (7 grams) instant yeast
2 teaspoons (6 grams) kosher salt
½ cup (122 grams) mashed cooked peeled russet potato (see Note)
½ cup (120 grams) plus 1 tablespoon (15 grams) whole milk, divided
¼ cup (57 grams) unsalted butter
¼ cup (60 grams) reserved potato cooking water (see Note) or water
2 large eggs (100 grams), divided

1. In the bowl of a stand mixer fitted with the paddle attachment, combine 1½ cups (188 grams) flour, sugar, yeast, and salt.
2. In a medium saucepan, heat mashed potato, ½ cup (120 grams) milk, butter, and ¼ cup (60 grams) potato water or water over medium heat, stirring occasionally, until an instant-read thermometer registers 120°F (49°C) to 130°F (54°C). Add hot potato mixture to flour mixture, and beat at medium speed until combined. Beat in 1 egg (50 grams) until combined. With mixer on low speed, gradually add 1¾ cups (219 grams) flour, beating just until combined and stopping to scrape sides of bowl.
3. Switch to the dough hook attachment. Beat at low speed until a soft, somewhat sticky dough forms, 10 to 12 minutes; add up to remaining ¼ cup (31 grams) flour, 1 tablespoon (8 grams) at a time, if dough is too sticky. Turn out dough onto a lightly floured surface, and shape into a smooth round.
4. Lightly oil a large bowl. Place dough in bowl, turning to grease top. Cover and let rise in a warm, draft-free place (75°F/24°C) until doubled in size, 45 minutes to 1 hour.
5. Line a rimmed baking sheet with parchment paper.
6. Turn out dough onto a lightly floured surface. Divide into 6 portions (about 138 grams each). Shape each portion into a round. Place rounds, seam side down, at least 2 inches apart on prepared pan. Cover and let rise in a warm, draft-free place (75°F/24°C) until doubled in size, about 1 hour.
7. Preheat oven to 350°F (180°C).
8. In a small bowl, whisk together remaining 1 egg (50 grams) and remaining 1 tablespoon (15 grams) milk. Gently brush egg wash on top of dough. Using a sharp paring knife or lame, score an "X" shape into top.
9. Bake until golden brown and an instant-read thermometer inserted in center registers 190°F (88°C), 20 to 25 minutes. Let cool on pan for 15 minutes. Remove from pan, and let cool completely on a wire rack. Store in an airtight container for up to 5 days, or tightly wrap in plastic wrap, and freeze for up to 3 months.

Note: *You can use leftover plain (no salt, butter, or other stir-ins) mashed potatoes, or boil peeled potatoes until fork-tender and then drain, reserving the cooking water for the dough, and mash.*

Ciabatta Rolls

Makes 8 rolls

The large, open crumb that's characteristic of ciabatta bread comes from a high hydration level in the dough as well as a poolish, which is a type of preferment (a fermentation starter or, sometimes, a "mother dough") that gives bread a slightly nutty flavor and thin crust. Pile these rolls high with salami, provolone, and other Italian ingredients for perfect panini.

Poolish:

1¼ cups plus 3 tablespoons (183 grams) bread flour
¾ cup plus 1 tablespoon (195 grams) room temperature water (70°F/21°C)
2 tablespoons (16 grams) all-purpose flour
1/16 teaspoon instant yeast

Dough:

1 cup (240 grams) cool water (60°F/16°C)
2 tablespoons (28 grams) olive oil
½ teaspoon instant yeast
2½ cups (318 grams) bread flour
½ cup (63 grams) all-purpose flour
1 tablespoon (9 grams) kosher salt

1. For poolish: In a medium bowl, stir together bread flour, ¾ cup plus 1 tablespoon (195 grams) water, all-purpose flour, and yeast until dry ingredients are completely moistened. Cover with plastic wrap, and let stand at room temperature for 14 to 16 hours.
2. For dough: In the bowl of a stand mixer fitted with the paddle attachment, place poolish. Add 1 cup (240 grams) water, oil, and yeast. Add flours and salt, and beat at low speed for 4 minutes.
3. Switch to the dough hook attachment. Beat at medium speed until dough gathers around dough hook and begins to pull away from sides of bowl, 8 to 10 minutes.
4. Oil a large bowl. Place dough in bowl, turning to grease top. Cover with plastic wrap, and let rise in a warm, draft-free place (75°F/24°C) for 1½ hours, folding dough in bowl after 30 minutes and again after 1 hour. (To fold, use a floured hand to reach under one side of dough, and pull gently over center. Repeat so all four sides of dough are folded; see Turn to Knead on page 30.)
5. Line a rimmed baking sheet with parchment paper.
6. Lightly dust work surface with all-purpose flour; turn out dough onto prepared surface, and shape into a 12x6-inch rectangle. Using a bench scraper, cut dough into 8 portions (about 3-inch squares). Carefully transfer dough to prepared pan, lightly stretching dough as needed for even sides. Cover and let rise in a warm, draft-free place (75°F/24°C) until puffed and dough holds an indentation when pressed, 1 to 1½ hours.
7. Preheat oven to 425°F (220°C).
8. Bake until golden brown and an instant-read thermometer inserted in center registers 205°F (96°C), 12 to 15 minutes. Let cool completely on wire racks. Store in an airtight container for up 5 days, or tightly wrap in plastic wrap, and freeze for up to 3 months.

Parker House Rolls

Makes 24 rolls

Everything is better with butter, and these Parker House Rolls are no exception. In this slight twist on the classic, pillowy rectangles of enriched dough get a brush of aromatic garlic butter before being shaped into their famed fold, brushed with a little more butter, and baked to golden perfection. Finished with a final coating of garlic butter punctuated with fresh parsley, these rolls are a timeless New England classic you'll bake again and again.

Dough:

- ½ **cup (120 grams) warm water (110°F/43°C to 115°F/46°C)**
- 5 **tablespoons (60 grams) granulated sugar, divided**
- 1½ **tablespoons (14 grams) active dry yeast**
- 1¼ **cups (300 grams) warm whole milk (110°F/43°C to 115°F/46°C)**
- ¼ **cup (57 grams) unsalted butter, melted and warm (110°F/43°C to 115°F/46°C)**
- 1 **large egg (50 grams), room temperature**
- 5 **cups (625 grams) all-purpose flour**
- 4 **teaspoons (12 grams) kosher salt**

Garlic butter:

- ⅓ **cup (76 grams) unsalted butter**
- ¾ **teaspoon granulated garlic**
- ½ **teaspoon kosher salt**

- 1 **tablespoon (2 grams) chopped fresh parsley**

1. For dough: In the bowl of a stand mixer, whisk together ½ cup (120 grams) warm water, 2 teaspoons (8 grams) sugar, and yeast by hand. Let stand until foamy, about 5 minutes. Whisk in warm milk, melted butter, and egg.
2. In a medium bowl, whisk together 5 cups (625 grams) flour, salt, and remaining 4 tablespoons plus 1 teaspoon (52 grams) sugar. Add flour mixture to yeast mixture; using the paddle attachment, beat at low speed until dough comes together.
3. Switch to the dough hook attachment. Beat at low speed until a smooth, elastic, somewhat sticky dough forms, 12 to 14 minutes, stopping to scrape sides of bowl and dough hook; add up to ¼ cup (31 grams) flour, 1 tablespoon (8 grams) at a time, if dough is too sticky. (Dough may still stick slightly to the bottom of the bowl but should pass the windowpane test; see page 16.) Turn out dough onto a very lightly floured surface, and gently shape into a ball.
4. Lightly oil a large bowl. Place dough in bowl, turning to grease top. Cover and let rise in a warm, draft-free place (75°F/24°C) until doubled in size, 30 to 45 minutes.
5. Punch down dough, and let stand for 10 minutes.
6. For garlic butter: In a small saucepan, heat all ingredients over medium heat, stirring occasionally, until fragrant, butter is melted, and salt dissolves, 2 to 3 minutes. Keep warm, but not hot, for use.
7. Preheat oven to 350°F (180°C). Butter a 13x9-inch baking pan.
8. Turn out dough onto a lightly floured surface, and shape into a rectangle with your hands. Roll dough into a 16x12-inch rectangle. Using a sharp knife or a pastry wheel, cut into 24 (4x2-inch) rectangles. Working with 1 rectangle at time, brush garlic butter onto dough. Fold rectangle crosswise so top portion hangs over bottom portion by about ¼ inch. Place in prepared pan. Repeat with remaining dough and garlic butter, shingling rolls as they are placed in pan (4 rows of 6). Cover and let rise in a warm, draft-free place (75°F/24°C) until puffed, 10 to 20 minutes.
9. Brush dough with garlic butter.
10. Bake until golden brown and an instant-read thermometer inserted in center registers 190°F (88°C), 20 to 25 minutes, rotating pan halfway through baking.
11. Stir parsley into garlic butter; brush onto hot rolls. Best served warm. Store in an airtight container for up to 3 days.

Fluffy Dinner Rolls

Makes 12 rolls

These soft rolls are a delightful centerpiece for any meal, boasting a light, fluffy texture that's elevated by the distinct flavor of yeast. The use of both sour cream and butter adds richness to the dough, ensuring each roll has a golden, tender crumb. The finishing touch of flaked sea salt offers a perfect contrast to the rolls' sweetness, making each bite a little burst of savory delight.

4¾ to 5 cups (594 to 625 grams) all-purpose flour, divided
¼ cup (50 grams) granulated sugar
1½ tablespoons (14 grams) instant yeast
1 tablespoon (9 grams) kosher salt
1 cup (240 grams) plus 1 tablespoon (15 grams) water, divided
½ cup (120 grams) sour cream
⅓ cup (76 grams) plus 2 tablespoons (28 grams) unsalted butter, melted and divided
2 large eggs (100 grams), room temperature and divided
Garnish: flaked sea salt

1. In the bowl of a stand mixer, whisk together 1½ cups (188 grams) flour, sugar, yeast, and kosher salt by hand.
2. In a small saucepan, heat 1 cup (240 grams) water, sour cream, and ⅓ cup (76 grams) melted butter over medium heat until an instant-read thermometer registers 120°F (49°C) to 130°F (54°C). Add hot sour cream mixture to flour mixture; using the paddle attachment, beat at medium speed until combined. Beat in 1 egg (50 grams) until combined. With mixer on low speed, gradually add 3¼ cups (406 grams) flour, beating just until a shaggy dough forms.
3. Switch to the dough hook attachment. Beat at low speed until a soft, somewhat sticky dough forms, 10 to 12 minutes, stopping to scrape dough hook and bottom and sides of bowl; add up to remaining ¼ cup (31 grams) flour, 1 tablespoon (8 grams) at a time, if dough is too sticky. Cover and let stand in a warm, draft-free place (75°F/24°C) until dough is puffed up, 20 to 30 minutes.
4. Line a 13x9-inch baking pan with parchment paper.
5. Divide dough into 12 portions (about 97 grams each). Using lightly floured hands, roll 1 portion into a smooth ball. (Keep remaining dough covered to prevent it from drying out.) Place in prepared pan. Repeat with remaining dough portions. Cover and let rise in a warm, draft-free place (75°F/24°C) until doubled in size, 30 to 40 minutes.
6. Preheat oven to 375°F (190°C).
7. In a small bowl, whisk together remaining 1 egg (50 grams) and remaining 1 tablespoon (15 grams) water; brush onto dough. Garnish with sea salt, if desired.
8. Bake until golden brown and an instant-read thermometer inserted in center registers 190°F (88°C), 18 to 22 minutes, covering with foil to prevent excess browning, if necessary. Let cool in pan for 10 minutes. Brush remaining 2 tablespoons (28 grams) melted butter onto rolls. Best served warm. Store in an airtight container for up to 3 days.

Garlic Breadsticks

Makes 24 breadsticks

Doused with melted butter, garlic salt, and Italian seasoning, these tender breadsticks pay homage to a famed restaurant chain's unlimited golden-brown batons.

5½ to 5¾ cups (688 to 719 grams) all-purpose flour, divided
¼ cup (50 grams) granulated sugar
4¼ teaspoons (13 grams) kosher salt
2¼ teaspoons (7 grams) instant yeast
1⅓ cups (320 grams) plus 1 tablespoon (15 grams) water, divided
½ cup (120 grams) whole milk
¼ cup (56 grams) olive oil
2 tablespoons (28 grams) unsalted butter
1 large egg (50 grams), lightly beaten
¼ cup (57 grams) unsalted butter, melted
½ teaspoon garlic salt
½ teaspoon dried Italian seasoning
Freshly grated Parmesan cheese, for topping

1. In the bowl of a stand mixer fitted with the paddle attachment, beat 2 cups (250 grams) flour, sugar, kosher salt, and yeast at medium-low speed just until combined.

2. In a medium saucepan, combine 1⅓ cups (320 grams) water, milk, oil, and butter; cook over medium heat, stirring frequently, until butter is melted and an instant-read thermometer registers 120°F (49°C) to 130°F (54°C). Add hot milk mixture to flour mixture; beat at medium-low speed until combined, about 1 minute, stopping to scrape sides of bowl. With mixer on low speed, gradually add 3½ cups (438 grams) flour, beating just until combined.

3. Switch to the dough hook attachment. Beat at medium-low speed until a soft, slightly sticky dough forms, 4 to 6 minutes, stopping to scrape dough hook and sides of bowl; add up to remaining ¼ cup (31 grams) flour, 1 tablespoon (8 grams) at a time, as needed if dough is too sticky. (Dough may still stick slightly to sides of bowl but should pass the windowpane test; see page 16.)

4. Spray a large bowl with cooking spray. Place dough in bowl, turning to grease top. Cover and let rise in a warm, draft-free place (75°F/24°C) until doubled in size, 40 minutes to 1 hour.

5. Line 3 rimmed baking sheets with parchment paper.

6. Punch down dough; cover and let stand for 10 minutes. On a clean surface, divide dough into 24 portions (about 51 grams each), and cover with a sheet of plastic wrap. Shape each portion into a ball; cover and let stand for 10 minutes. Gently flatten each ball to release large air bubbles; shape each portion into a 9- to 10-inch rope of even thickness, very lightly flouring surface or hands as needed. Place, seam side down, 1 inch apart on prepared pans. (Dough ropes will shrink to 7 to 8 inches.) Press in any pointed ends to make dough ropes more rounded, if necessary. Cover and let rise in a warm, draft-free place (75°F/24°C) until puffed and dough holds an indentation when pressed, 25 to 35 minutes.

7. Position oven rack in top third of oven. Preheat oven to 425°F (220°C).

8. In a small bowl, whisk together egg and remaining 1 tablespoon (15 grams) water; brush onto dough.

9. Bake, one pan at a time, until golden brown, 10 to 12 minutes. Let cool on pan for 5 minutes.

10. In another small bowl, stir together melted butter, garlic salt, and Italian seasoning; brush onto warm breadsticks. Sprinkle with cheese. Best served warm. Store in an airtight container for up to 2 days.

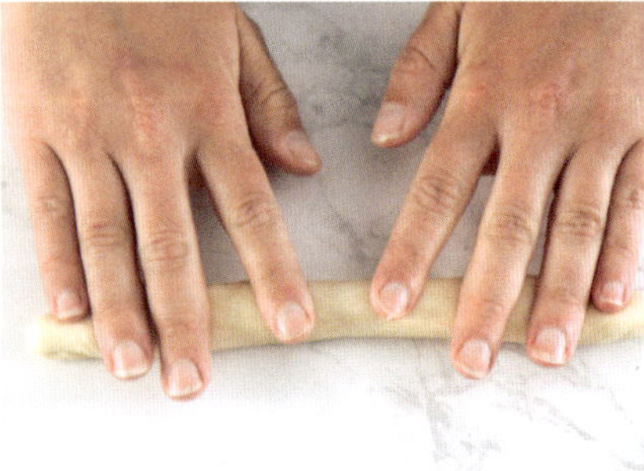

Hawaiian Rolls

Makes 15 rolls

From the lava rock-fashioned *fornos* of the 1800s to the industrial ovens of today, these iconic bread rolls continue to enchant all who taste them. This recipe keeps it simple and sweet, celebrating the pineapple juice-packed original in all its beauty.

---

2 tablespoons (30 grams) warm water (110°F/43°C to 115°F/46°C)
1 tablespoon (9 grams) active dry yeast
⅓ cup (73 grams) plus ¼ teaspoon firmly packed dark brown sugar, divided
¾ cup (180 grams) canned pineapple juice, room temperature
¼ cup (57 grams) unsalted butter, melted and cooled slightly
3 large eggs (150 grams), room temperature and divided
1 large egg yolk (19 grams), room temperature
1 teaspoon vanilla extract
4¼ cups (531 grams) all-purpose flour
1 tablespoon (9 grams) kosher salt
1 tablespoon (15 grams) water, room temperature
¼ cup (85 grams) clover honey
1 tablespoon (14 grams) unsalted butter

1. In the bowl of a stand mixer, whisk together 2 tablespoons (30 grams) warm water, yeast, and ¼ teaspoon brown sugar. Let stand until foamy, about 10 minutes.
2. Add pineapple juice, melted butter, 2 eggs (100 grams), egg yolk, vanilla, and remaining ⅓ cup (73 grams) brown sugar to yeast mixture; using the paddle attachment, beat at medium-low speed until well combined, stopping to scrape sides of bowl. With mixer on low speed, gradually add flour and salt, beating just until combined and stopping to scrape sides of bowl. Beat for 2 minutes. (Dough will still be quite rough.)
3. Switch to the dough hook attachment. Beat at low speed until dough is elastic and relatively smooth, 5 to 8 minutes, stopping to scrape dough hook and sides of bowl. (Dough will still stick to sides of bowl and should pass the windowpane test; see page 16.)
4. Spray a large bowl with cooking spray. Place dough in bowl, turning to grease top. Cover and let rise in a warm, draft-free place (75°F/24°C) until doubled in size, 1 to 2 hours.
5. Lightly spray a 13x9-inch baking pan with cooking spray. Line pan with parchment paper, letting excess extend over sides of pan.
6. Punch down dough; cover and let stand for 10 minutes. Divide dough into 15 portions (about 64 grams each). On a clean surface, roll portions into balls, and place, evenly spaced, in prepared pan. Cover and let rise in a warm, draft-free place (75°F/24°C) until nearly doubled in size and dough holds an indentation when pressed, 1 to 1½ hours.
7. Preheat oven to 350°F (180°C).
8. In a small bowl, whisk together 1 tablespoon (15 grams) room temperature water and remaining 1 egg (50 grams); gently brush egg wash onto dough.
9. Bake until golden brown, 20 to 25 minutes, loosely covering with foil during final 3 to 5 minutes of baking to prevent excess browning.
10. In a small microwave-safe bowl, combine honey and butter. Heat on high in 10-second intervals, stirring between each, until butter is melted and mixture is smooth. Brush rolls with honey glaze. Best served warm. Store in an airtight container for up to 3 days.

Sour Cream Fantails

Makes 12 rolls

These mini pull-aparts pack rich sour cream and bright green onion flavor in every layer.

3¼ to 3½ cups (406 to 437 grams) all-purpose flour, divided
3 tablespoons (36 grams) granulated sugar
1 tablespoon (9 grams) plus ¼ teaspoon kosher salt, divided
2¼ teaspoons (7 grams) instant yeast
1 teaspoon garlic powder, divided
¼ teaspoon baking soda
¾ cup (180 grams) plus 1 tablespoon (15 grams) water, divided
½ cup (120 grams) sour cream
8 tablespoons (112 grams) unsalted butter, cubed and divided
½ cup (55 grams) plus 1 tablespoon (7 grams) finely chopped green onion, divided
1 large egg (50 grams)

1. In the bowl of a stand mixer fitted with the paddle attachment, beat 1 cup (125 grams) flour, sugar, 1 tablespoon (9 grams) salt, yeast, ½ teaspoon garlic powder, and baking soda at low speed until combined.
2. In a medium saucepan, heat ¾ cup (180 grams) water, sour cream, and 3 tablespoons (42 grams) butter over medium-low heat, stirring frequently, until butter is melted and an instant-read thermometer registers 120°F (49°C) to 130°F (54°C). Add hot sour cream mixture to flour mixture; beat at medium-low speed until combined, about 1 minute, stopping to scrape sides of bowl. With mixer on low speed, gradually add 2¼ cups (281 grams) flour and ½ cup (55 grams) green onion, beating just until combined and stopping to scrape sides of bowl.
3. Switch to the dough hook attachment. Beat at low speed until a soft, somewhat sticky dough forms, 10 to 12 minutes, stopping to scrape dough hook and sides of bowl; add up to remaining ¼ cup (31 grams) flour, 1 tablespoon (8 grams) at a time, if dough is too sticky. (Dough will mostly pull away from sides of bowl and should pass the windowpane test; see page 16.) Turn out dough onto a lightly floured surface, and shape into a smooth round.
4. Lightly oil a large bowl. Place dough in bowl, turning to grease top. Cover and let rise in a warm, draft-free place (75°F/24°C) until doubled in size, 30 to 45 minutes.
5. Punch down dough; cover and let stand for 10 minutes.
6. Spray a 12-cup muffin pan with cooking spray.
7. In a small microwave-safe bowl, heat remaining 5 tablespoons (70 grams) butter on high in 10-second intervals until melted.
8. Divide dough in half. On a lightly floured surface, roll half of dough into a 12-inch square. (Keep remaining dough covered to prevent it from drying out.) Brush 1 tablespoon (14 grams) melted butter onto dough square. Using a pizza cutter, cut dough into 12 (6x2-inch) strips. Stack 6 strips, butter side up; repeat with remaining 6 strips to create a separate stack. Using a floured serrated knife, cut each stack crosswise into 3 (2-inch) squares. Place each square stack, layered side up, in prepared muffin cups. Repeat procedure with remaining dough and 1 tablespoon (14 grams) melted butter. Slightly separate layers of each fantail. Loosely cover with plastic wrap, and let rise in a warm, draft-free place (75°F/24°C) until dough fills cups, 15 to 25 minutes.
9. Preheat oven to 375°F (190°C).
10. In a small bowl, whisk together egg and remaining 1 tablespoon (15 grams) water; brush onto dough.
11. Bake until golden brown, 12 to 15 minutes.
12. Stir remaining 1 tablespoon (7 grams) green onion, remaining ½ teaspoon garlic powder, and remaining ¼ teaspoon salt into remaining melted butter; brush onto hot rolls. Let cool for 10 minutes. Best served warm. Store in an airtight container for up to 3 days.

MUFFINS and QUICK BREAD LOAVES

From cinnamon-swirled banana bread and fruity muffins to herb-infused soda bread and crispy-crusted cornbread, these breads rise and shine in minimal time

Apple Cider Doughnut Loaf

Makes 1 (8½x4½-inch) loaf

A crunchy sprinkle of cinnamon sugar simply but elegantly finishes this fragrant bread.

---

2 cups (480 grams) apple cider
¾ cup (168 grams) neutral oil
½ cup (100 grams) plus 3 tablespoons (36 grams) granulated sugar, divided
½ cup (120 grams) sour cream
⅓ cup (73 grams) firmly packed light brown sugar
1 large egg (50 grams), room temperature
1 teaspoon vanilla extract
2⅔ cups (333 grams) all-purpose flour
1 tablespoon (6 grams) apple pie spice
2 teaspoons (10 grams) baking powder
2 teaspoons ground cinnamon, divided
1½ teaspoons (5 grams) kosher salt
¼ teaspoon baking soda
1 teaspoon unsalted butter, room temperature
1 tablespoon (14 grams) unsalted butter, melted

1. In a medium saucepan, bring cider to a boil over medium-high heat; cook, stirring occasionally, until reduced to ¾ cup (181 grams), 15 to 20 minutes. Remove from heat, and let cool completely.
2. Preheat oven to 350°F (180°C). Spray an 8½x4½-inch loaf pan with baking spray with flour. Line pan with parchment paper, letting excess extend over sides of pan.
3. In a large bowl, whisk together oil, ½ cup (100 grams) granulated sugar, sour cream, brown sugar, egg, and vanilla.
4. In a medium bowl, whisk together flour, pie spice, baking powder, 1 teaspoon cinnamon, salt, and baking soda. Gradually add flour mixture to sugar mixture alternately with reduced cider, beginning and ending with flour mixture, whisking until just combined after each addition. Spread batter into prepared pan.
5. Spoon room temperature butter into a pastry bag, and cut a ¼-inch opening in tip. Pipe lengthwise down center of batter.
6. Bake until a wooden pick inserted in center comes out with a few moist crumbs, 1 hour to 1 hour and 5 minutes. Let cool in pan for 10 minutes. Using excess parchment as handles, remove from pan, and let cool completely on a wire rack.
7. Using a pastry brush, brush melted butter onto cooled loaf. In a small bowl, whisk together remaining 3 tablespoons (36 grams) granulated sugar and remaining 1 teaspoon cinnamon; sprinkle onto loaf. Let stand until butter has been absorbed into loaf. Store in an airtight container for up to 3 days.

PRO TIP: The line of butter on top of the batter helps create the signature domed rise and lengthwise crack in the top of a quick bread loaf—not to mention a little extra flavor!

Cinnamon Crunch Banana Bread

Makes 1 (8½x4½-inch) loaf

Just when you thought banana bread couldn't get any better, this moist, incredibly tender loaf takes all the comfort of the classic and adds a fun yet familiar twist of cinnamon sugar ribbons and crunchy spicy-sweet topping. Requiring only a few simple steps to make, this banana bread is bound to become a family favorite.

Filling:
2 tablespoons (16 grams) all-purpose flour
2 tablespoons (28 grams) firmly packed light brown sugar
2 teaspoons (4 grams) ground cinnamon
2 teaspoons (10 grams) unsalted butter, room temperature

Batter:
1⅔ cups (208 grams) all-purpose flour
¾ teaspoon kosher salt
½ teaspoon baking soda
¼ teaspoon baking powder
1 cup (240 grams) mashed ripe banana (about 3 medium bananas)
¾ cup (165 grams) firmly packed light brown sugar
¼ cup (56 grams) neutral oil
¼ cup (60 grams) sour cream, room temperature
2 large eggs (100 grams), room temperature
2 tablespoons (28 grams) unsalted butter, melted
1½ teaspoons (9 grams) vanilla bean paste

Cinnamon Sugar Topping (recipe follows)

1. Preheat oven to 325°F (170°C). Spray an 8½x4½-inch loaf pan with baking spray with flour. Line pan with parchment paper, letting excess extend over sides of pan.
2. For filling: In a small bowl, stir together flour, brown sugar, and cinnamon. Using your fingers, cut in butter until mixture is well combined and sandy.
3. For batter: In a medium bowl, whisk together flour, salt, baking soda, and baking powder.
4. In a large bowl, whisk together banana, brown sugar, oil, sour cream, eggs, melted butter, and vanilla bean paste. Gradually stir in flour mixture just until combined. Spread one-third of batter (about 1 cup or 280 grams) into prepared pan. Sprinkle half of filling (about 2½ packed tablespoons or 30 grams) on top, leaving a ⅛- to ¼-inch border around edges. Spread one-third of batter on top, and sprinkle remaining filling onto batter, leaving a ⅛- to ¼-inch border around edges. Dollop remaining batter on top, and spread into an even layer. Sprinkle Cinnamon Sugar Topping on top.
5. Bake for 40 minutes. Rotate pan, and bake until a wooden pick inserted in center comes out clean and an instant-read thermometer inserted in center registers 200°F (93°C) to 205°F (96°C), 26 to 32 minutes more, loosely covering with foil during final 10 to 12 minutes of baking to prevent excess browning. Let cool in pan on a wire rack for 10 minutes. Remove from pan, and let cool on wire rack for 10 minutes. Serve warm, or let cool completely.

Cinnamon Sugar Topping

Makes about 3 tablespoons

2 tablespoons (28 grams) firmly packed light brown sugar
1 teaspoon all-purpose flour
¼ teaspoon ground cinnamon
1 teaspoon cold unsalted butter

1. In a small bowl, stir together brown sugar, flour, and cinnamon. Using your fingers, cut in cold butter until mixture resembles coarse bread crumbs. Refrigerate until ready to use.

Pumpkin-Chocolate Swirl Bread

Makes 1 (8½x4½-inch) loaf

This beautifully marbled bake is as indulgent to eat as it is pretty to present.

1½ cups (188 grams) all-purpose flour
1 tablespoon (6 grams) pumpkin pie spice
2 teaspoons (10 grams) baking powder
1 teaspoon kosher salt
¼ teaspoon baking soda
1 cup (240 grams) canned pumpkin
½ cup (100 grams) granulated sugar
⅓ cup (73 grams) firmly packed light brown sugar
2 large eggs (100 grams), room temperature
3 tablespoons (42 grams) vegetable oil
1 teaspoon vanilla extract
½ cup (128 grams) hazelnut chocolate spread

1. Preheat oven to 350°F (180°C). Spray an 8½x4½-inch loaf pan with baking spray with flour. Line pan with parchment paper, letting excess extend over sides of pan.
2. In a medium bowl, whisk together flour, pie spice, baking powder, salt, and baking soda.
3. In a large bowl, whisk together pumpkin, sugars, eggs, oil, and vanilla until smooth. Whisk in flour mixture until thick and smooth. Spread half of batter (about 1¼ cups or 375 grams) into prepared pan.
4. Spoon hazelnut chocolate spread into a pastry bag, and cut a ¼-inch opening in tip. Pipe half of spread evenly onto batter, leaving a ¼-inch border around edges. Using an offset spatula or skewer, gently swirl together spread and batter, avoiding sides of pan. Repeat procedure with remaining batter and remaining hazelnut chocolate spread.
5. Bake until a wooden pick inserted in center comes out with a few moist crumbs, 50 to 55 minutes. Let cool in pan for 10 minutes. Using excess parchment as handles, remove from pan, and let cool completely on a wire rack. Store in an airtight container for up to 3 days.

Double-Chocolate Zucchini Muffins

Makes 12 muffins

Why go for zucchini bread when you could have these indulgent muffins? Owing their soft texture to juicy zucchini, these muffins get a dose of decadence from white chocolate chips embedded in the cocoa-rich batter.

- 1 cup (200 grams) granulated sugar
- ½ cup (120 grams) sour cream, room temperature
- ⅓ cup (76 grams) unsalted butter, melted
- ⅓ cup (80 grams) whole milk, room temperature
- 2 large eggs (100 grams), room temperature
- 1 teaspoon vanilla extract
- 2 cups (250 grams) all-purpose flour
- ½ cup (43 grams) Dutch process cocoa powder
- 1½ teaspoons (8 grams) baking powder
- ½ teaspoon baking soda
- ½ teaspoon kosher salt
- 1 cup (120 grams) shredded zucchini, patted dry
- 1 cup (170 grams) white chocolate chips

1. Preheat oven 350°F (180°C). Line a 12-cup muffin pan with tall-sided parchment paper liners.
2. In a large bowl, whisk together sugar, sour cream, melted butter, and milk; whisk in eggs and vanilla.
3. In a medium bowl, whisk together flour, cocoa, baking powder, baking soda, and salt. Add flour mixture to sugar mixture, whisking just until combined. Fold in zucchini and white chocolate chips. Divide batter among prepared muffin cups.
4. Bake until a wooden pick inserted in center comes out clean and an instant-read thermometer inserted in center registers 205°F (96°C) to 210°F (99°C), 20 to 25 minutes. Let cool in pan for 10 minutes. Remove from pan, and serve warm, or let cool completely on a wire rack.

Make Your Own Parchment Paper Muffin Liners

For every liner you need, cut out a 6-inch square of parchment paper.

Fold square in half one direction; unfold, and fold in half the other direction. The paper should be folded into quarters.

Place the center of the square on the top of a 6-ounce can or the bottom of a cup with a 2-inch diameter. Run your hands along the sides of the can or cup and over the parchment to create deep folds.

Run your finger around the rim of the can or cup bottom to mold the parchment into a round shape.

Remove the parchment, and place in the muffin pan.

Strawberry-Ricotta Muffins

Makes 12 muffins

Topped with a crunchy streusel, these muffins aren't just a great on-the-go breakfast; they're an indulgent snack, a fruity dessert, or an elegant brunch bread. A combination of melted butter and oil creates a moist crumb, creamy ricotta adds richness, and sweet strawberries provide a burst of fresh flavor to every bite.

Batter:
3 cups (376 grams) all-purpose flour, divided
2 teaspoons (10 grams) baking powder
1½ teaspoons (5 grams) kosher salt
½ teaspoon baking soda
1 cup (200 grams) granulated sugar
1 cup (225 grams) whole-milk ricotta cheese
¼ cup (57 grams) unsalted butter, melted
¼ cup (56 grams) neutral oil
3 large eggs (150 grams), room temperature
2 teaspoons (8 grams) vanilla extract
1¾ cups (301 grams) chopped fresh strawberries, patted dry

Topping:
2 cups (250 grams) all-purpose flour
6 tablespoons (72 grams) granulated sugar
6 tablespoons (84 grams) firmly packed light brown sugar
1½ teaspoons (5 grams) kosher salt
¾ cup (170 grams) unsalted butter, melted
1½ teaspoons (6 grams) vanilla extract
¼ cup (44 grams) chopped fresh strawberries
2 tablespoons (24 grams) turbinado sugar

Strawberry preserves, to serve

1. For batter: In a large bowl, whisk together 2¾ cups plus 2 tablespoons (360 grams) flour, baking powder, salt, and baking soda.
2. In a medium bowl, whisk together granulated sugar, ricotta, melted butter, oil, eggs, and vanilla until well combined. Add sugar mixture to flour mixture, folding just until dry ingredients are moistened.
3. In another medium bowl, toss together strawberries and remaining 2 tablespoons (16 grams) flour; stir into batter just until combined. (Batter will be lumpy; do not overmix.) Cover and refrigerate for 1 hour, or up to overnight.
4. For topping: In another medium bowl, whisk together flour, granulated sugar, brown sugar, and salt until well combined. Stir in melted butter and vanilla until mixture is well combined and crumbly. Cover and refrigerate.
5. Preheat oven to 400°F (200°C). Line every other cup of 2 (12-cup) muffin pans with tall-sided parchment paper liners. Fill empty cups halfway with water.
6. Divide batter among prepared muffin cups (about ½ cup or 115 grams each).
7. Bake for 5 minutes. Reduce oven temperature to 375°F (190°C), and bake for 5 minutes more. Working quickly, sprinkle ¼ cup (36 grams) lightly packed topping mixture onto each muffin. Sprinkle strawberries and turbinado sugar on top. Bake until a wooden pick inserted in center comes out clean, 13 to 15 minutes more. Let cool in pans on wire racks for 15 minutes. Serve warm with preserves. Store in an airtight container for up to 3 days.

PRO TIPS: Refrigerating the batter allows the flour to fully hydrate, which leads to a higher rise during baking. Batter can also be refrigerated overnight for a make-ahead option.

Tall-sided parchment paper liners allow the muffins to bake up high with a nice dome and straight sides.

WILLIAMS-

Bakery-Style Blueberry Muffins

Makes 12 muffins

I've long been a fan of Michelle Lopez of *Hummingbird High* and her techniques for fruit-filled, high-rising muffins, which influenced my creation of this dreamy recipe: a heaping helping of both whole and smashed fresh blueberries, lemon zest and juice for brightness, turbinado sugar for a crunchy top, sour cream and oil for a moist crumb, and a gorgeously domed top.

- **3 cups (376 grams) all-purpose flour, divided**
- **1 tablespoon (15 grams) baking powder**
- **1½ teaspoons (5 grams) kosher salt**
- **1 cup (200 grams) granulated sugar**
- **1 cup (240 grams) sour cream, room temperature**
- **3 large eggs (150 grams), room temperature**
- **¼ cup (57 grams) unsalted butter, melted**
- **¼ cup (56 grams) neutral oil**
- **1 tablespoon (3 grams) lemon zest**
- **2 tablespoons (30 grams) fresh lemon juice**
- **2 teaspoons (8 grams) vanilla extract**
- **2½ cups (350 grams) fresh blueberries, divided**
- **2 tablespoons (24 grams) turbinado sugar**

1. In a large bowl, whisk together 2¾ cups plus 2 tablespoons (360 grams) flour, baking powder, and salt.
2. In a medium bowl, whisk together granulated sugar, sour cream, eggs, melted butter, oil, lemon zest and juice, and vanilla until well combined. Fold sugar mixture into flour mixture just until dry ingredients are moistened and some dry streaks remain.
3. In a small bowl, mash ½ cup (70 grams) blueberries with a fork.
4. In another medium bowl, stir together 1¾ cups (245 grams) blueberries and remaining 2 tablespoons (16 grams) flour. Fold mashed blueberries and blueberry mixture into batter just until combined. (Batter should still be lumpy; do not overmix.) Cover and refrigerate for at least 1 hour or up to overnight.
5. Preheat oven to 400°F (200°C). Spray 2 (12-cup) muffin pans with baking spray with flour. Fill every other muffin cup with water.
6. Divide batter among prepared muffin cups (about ½ cup or 118 grams each), spreading into an even layer. Top with remaining ¼ cup (35 grams) blueberries, pressing into batter. Sprinkle with turbinado sugar.
7. Bake for 5 minutes. Reduce oven temperature to 375°F (190°C), and bake until a wooden pick inserted in center comes out clean, 12 to 17 minutes more. Let cool in pans on wire racks for 10 minutes. Gently twist and loosen each muffin; leave muffins in cups, and let cool for 5 minutes. Serve warm. Store in an airtight container for up to 3 days.

PRO TIPS: Starting with a high oven temperature guarantees the muffins rise quickly and bake with a beautiful top and a tender interior.

When you alternate filling every other muffin cup with batter, there's enough room for the muffins to have rounded tops and crispy edges without crowding each other, and this step also ensures they bake evenly.

Smashing a handful of blueberries before adding them to the muffin batter creates a fruity burst in every bite.

Resting the batter allows the starch in the flour to absorb the liquids, resulting in a thick batter that holds its shape.

Don't skip spraying the muffin pan and its edges with baking spray with flour. When the muffins come out of the oven and rest for a few minutes, use a small offset spatula to gently loosen and release their edges from the pan. This helps the muffins come out of the pan cleanly without sticking.

Sourdough Discard Banana Bread

Makes 1 (8½x4½-inch) loaf

Sourdough discard adds depth and tenderness to this classic banana bread. Because discard isn't responsible for the primary lift, baking powder provides the leavening. The discard's subtle tang balances the sweetness of ripe bananas and brown sugar, adding complexity to this comforting quick bread.

- 2 cups (250 grams) all-purpose flour
- 2 teaspoons (10 grams) baking powder
- 1½ teaspoons (5 grams) kosher salt
- 1¼ cups (300 grams) mashed ripe banana (about 3 medium bananas)
- 1¼ cups (275 grams) firmly packed light brown sugar
- ½ cup (112 grams) neutral oil
- 2 large eggs (100 grams), room temperature
- 1 tablespoon (13 grams) vanilla extract
- ¾ cup (190 grams) Sourdough Starter discard (recipe and technique on page 68)

1. Preheat oven to 325°F (170°C). Spray a tall-sided 8½x4½-inch loaf pan with baking spray with flour. Line pan with parchment paper, letting excess extend over sides of pan.

2. In a medium bowl, whisk together flour, baking powder, and salt.

3. In a large bowl, whisk together banana, brown sugar, oil, eggs, and vanilla. Gradually stir in flour mixture and sourdough discard just until combined. Spread batter into prepared pan.

4. Bake for 1 hour. Rotate pan, and bake until a wooden pick inserted in center comes out clean and an instant-read thermometer inserted in center registers 200°F (93°C) to 205°F (96°C), 20 to 30 minutes more, loosely covering with foil during final 20 minutes of baking to prevent excess browning. Let cool in pan on a wire rack for 10 minutes. Using excess parchment as handles, remove from pan, and let cool completely on wire rack. Store in airtight container for up to 3 days.

Lemon-Poppy Seed Streusel Bread

Makes 1 (8½x4½-inch) loaf

The delicate crunch of the streusel topping gives way to an aromatic, soft crumb. With added texture from the poppy seeds, you won't be able to get enough of this loaf. It's great for breakfast, brunch, dessert, or an anytime treat.

Streusel:

¼ cup (31 grams) all-purpose flour
2 teaspoons (8 grams) granulated sugar
1 teaspoon poppy seeds
1½ tablespoons (21 grams) cold unsalted butter

Batter:

1¼ cups (250 grams) granulated sugar
3 tablespoons (9 grams) lemon zest
½ cup (113 grams) unsalted butter, softened
3 large eggs (150 grams), room temperature
½ teaspoon vanilla extract
2¼ cups (281 grams) all-purpose flour
1½ tablespoons (14 grams) poppy seeds
2 teaspoons (10 grams) baking powder
½ teaspoon kosher salt
½ cup (120 grams) buttermilk, room temperature
2 tablespoons (30 grams) fresh lemon juice

1. For streusel: In a medium bowl, whisk together flour, sugar, and poppy seeds. Using a pastry blender or 2 forks, cut in cold butter until incorporated and mixture is crumbly. Refrigerate until ready to use, at least 30 minutes.

2. Preheat oven to 375°F (190°C). Spray an 8½x4½-inch loaf pan with baking spray with flour. Line pan with parchment paper, letting excess extend over all sides of pan.

3. For batter: In the bowl of a stand mixer, whisk together sugar and lemon zest by hand until sugar is fragrant. Add butter; using the paddle attachment, beat at medium speed until light and fluffy, 3 to 4 minutes, stopping to scrape bottom and sides of bowl. Add eggs, one at a time, beating well after each addition and stopping to scrape sides of bowl. Beat in vanilla.

4. In another medium bowl, whisk together flour, poppy seeds, baking powder, and salt. In a small bowl, whisk together buttermilk and lemon juice. With mixer on low speed, gradually add flour mixture to sugar mixture alternately with buttermilk mixture, beginning and ending with flour mixture, beating just until combined after each addition. Spread batter into prepared pan. Firmly tap pan on a kitchen towel-lined counter to settle batter. Top batter with streusel.

5. Bake for 20 minutes. Reduce oven temperature to 350°F (180°C), and bake until a wooden pick inserted in center comes out with a few moist crumbs and an instant-read thermometer inserted in center registers at least 205°F (96°C), 50 to 55 minutes more. Let cool in pan for 15 minutes. Using excess parchment as handles, remove from pan, and let cool completely on a wire rack. Store in an airtight container for up to 3 days.

Spiced Pumpkin Bread

Makes 1 (8½x4½-inch) loaf

Maximum flavor and a soft texture for days were my top goals for this bread, and I more than succeeded. In addition to the fragrant blend of cinnamon, ginger, nutmeg, and cloves that comprises pumpkin pie spice, a pinch of black pepper adds a faintly lingering touch of heat. Dark brown sugar's higher molasses content brings a caramelly depth of flavor and moisture, and vanilla extract adds floral sweetness. Using oil rather than butter lets the pumpkin flavor shine while keeping the crumb tender; plus, it helps create the cracked dome on top, the instantly recognizable sign of a quick bread. Enjoy thick slices of this easy loaf for breakfast, an afternoon snack, or dessert.

2½ cups (313 grams) all-purpose flour
1 tablespoon plus 2 teaspoons (10 grams) pumpkin pie spice
2 teaspoons (10 grams) baking powder
2 teaspoons (6 grams) kosher salt
½ teaspoon ground black pepper
1 (15-ounce) can (425 grams) pumpkin
1 cup (200 grams) granulated sugar
⅔ cup (149 grams) neutral oil, plus more for scoring
½ cup (110 grams) firmly packed dark brown sugar
2 large eggs (100 grams), room temperature
2 teaspoons (8 grams) vanilla extract

1. Preheat oven to 325°F (170°C). Spray an 8½x4½-inch loaf pan with baking spray with flour. Line pan with parchment paper, letting excess extend over all sides of pan.

2. In a large bowl, whisk together flour, pie spice, baking powder, salt, and pepper.

3. In a medium bowl, whisk together pumpkin, granulated sugar, oil, brown sugar, eggs, and vanilla until smooth. Fold pumpkin mixture into flour mixture until smooth. Spread batter into prepared pan. Firmly tap pan on a kitchen towel-lined counter to settle batter. Using an offset spatula dipped in oil, score a line lengthwise down center of batter, leaving about a 1-inch border on short sides of pan.

4. Bake until a wooden pick inserted in center comes out with a few moist crumbs, 1½ hours to 1 hour and 40 minutes. Let cool in pan for 10 minutes. Using excess parchment as handles, remove from pan, and let cool completely on a wire rack. Store in an airtight container for up to 3 days.

Classic Southern Cornbread

Makes 1 (10-inch) loaf

Throughout the American South, where I was born and raised, people debate whether cornbread should be sweet or savory and what type of baking pan or dish is best. I prefer a savory version, but for me, there is no debating that cornbread should be baked in a preheated greased cast-iron skillet. It's the essential step to creating a crunchy, uniformly golden-brown bottom crust—as is eating cornbread immediately out of the oven so steam doesn't accumulate in the skillet and soften the crust.

- **¼ cup (56 grams) canola oil**
- **2 cups (300 grams) plain cornmeal (see Note)**
- **1 cup (125 grams) all-purpose flour**
- **1 tablespoon (15 grams) baking powder**
- **1½ teaspoons (5 grams) kosher salt**
- **2½ cups (600 grams) buttermilk, room temperature**
- **6 tablespoons (84 grams) unsalted butter, melted**
- **2 large eggs (100 grams), room temperature**

1. Preheat oven to 425°F (220°C). Pour oil into a 10-inch cast-iron skillet. Place skillet in oven while oven preheats.
2. In a large bowl, whisk together cornmeal, flour, baking powder, and salt. Make a well in center.
3. In a medium bowl, whisk together buttermilk, melted butter, and eggs. Add buttermilk mixture to cornmeal mixture, and stir just until combined. Carefully pour batter into hot skillet. (Batter should sizzle around sides of skillet.)
4. Bake until golden brown and a wooden pick inserted in center comes out clean, about 25 minutes. Serve immediately. Store in an airtight container for up to 2 days.

Note: *Be sure you're using plain cornmeal rather than cornmeal mix or cornbread mix, both of which have flour, leavening, and salt already added. Use any color of cornmeal you like.*

Beer-Cheddar Muffins

Makes 12 muffins

All during my childhood and teen years, my mother made these for our family suppers, and my twin brother and I used to fight over who got to have more muffins. After just one bite, you'll understand why this recipe has been in my family's regular rotation for decades.

1½ cups (188 grams) all-purpose flour
1¼ cups (156 grams) unbleached cake flour
5 teaspoons (20 grams) granulated sugar
1¾ teaspoons (5 grams) kosher salt
1¾ teaspoons (3 grams) chopped fresh rosemary
1½ teaspoons (8 grams) baking powder
1½ teaspoons (3 grams) ground black pepper
½ teaspoon baking soda
¾ cup (170 grams) cold unsalted butter, cubed
1 cup (240 grams) cold lager beer
¾ cup (85 grams) shredded sharp white Cheddar cheese

1. Preheat oven to 400°F (200°C). Spray a 12-cup muffin pan with baking spray with flour.
2. In a large bowl, whisk together flours, sugar, salt, rosemary, baking powder, pepper, and baking soda. Using a pastry blender or 2 forks, cut in cold butter until mixture resembles coarse crumbs. Gradually add cold beer, stirring just until dry ingredients are moistened. Fold in cheese until well combined. (Dough will be sticky and wet.)
3. Using a 3-tablespoon spring-loaded scoop, scoop batter into prepared muffin cups (about 73 grams each).
4. Bake until edges are golden brown, 15 to 18 minutes. Let cool in pan for 5 minutes. Best served warm. Store in an airtight container for up to 3 days.

Parmesan-Herb Buttermilk Bread

Makes 1 (8½x4½-inch) loaf

The flavors of ranch dressing—buttermilk, herbs, onion, and garlic—come together in this deliciously cheesy quick bread. Serve slices warm with butter or top with your favorite fillings for an open-faced sandwich.

2½ cups (313 grams) all-purpose flour
1 tablespoon (12 grams) granulated sugar
1½ teaspoons (8 grams) baking powder
1 teaspoon kosher salt
1 teaspoon garlic powder
1 teaspoon onion powder
¼ teaspoon baking soda
⅛ teaspoon ground red pepper
⅛ teaspoon ground black pepper
1¼ cups (100 grams) shredded Parmesan cheese, divided
¼ cup (5 grams) lightly packed chopped fresh parsley
2 tablespoons (5 grams) lightly packed chopped fresh dill
1⅓ cups (320 grams) buttermilk, room temperature
⅓ cup (76 grams) unsalted butter, melted
1 large egg (50 grams), room temperature
Garnish: chopped fresh parsley, chopped fresh dill

1. Preheat oven to 350°F (180°C). Spray an 8½x4½-inch loaf pan with baking spray with flour. Line pan with parchment paper, letting excess extend over sides of pan.
2. In a large bowl, stir together flour, sugar, baking powder, salt, garlic powder, onion powder, baking soda, and peppers. Whisk in 1 cup (80 grams) cheese, parsley, and dill.
3. In another large bowl, whisk together buttermilk, melted butter, and egg. Add flour mixture, stirring until just combined. Pour batter into prepared pan; sprinkle 2 tablespoons (10 grams) cheese on top.
4. Bake until a wooden pick inserted in center comes out clean and an instant-read thermometer inserted in center registers 200°F (93°C), 50 to 55 minutes. Sprinkle with remaining 2 tablespoons (10 grams) cheese; garnish with parsley and dill, if desired.
5. Let cool in pan for 5 minutes. Using excess parchment as handles, remove from pan, and let cool on a wire rack for at least 15 minutes. Serve warm or at room temperature.

Irish White Cheddar Soda Bread

Makes 1 (10-inch) loaf

Slashed with a cross and pricked to release heat, my take on traditional soda bread is enhanced with strong Irish Cheddar, fresh dill, and ground black pepper.

3⅔ cups (458 grams) all-purpose flour
1½ teaspoons (5 grams) kosher salt
½ teaspoon baking soda
1 cup (113 grams) shredded aged Irish white Cheddar cheese, divided
1 tablespoon (2 grams) chopped fresh dill
½ teaspoon ground black pepper
2 cups (480 grams) buttermilk

1. Preheat oven to 450°F (230°C).
2. In a large bowl, whisk together flour, salt, and baking soda until well combined. Stir in ⅔ cup (75 grams) cheese, dill, and pepper. Make a well in center, and add buttermilk. Using your hand like a claw, mix buttermilk into dry ingredients, working from center to outside of bowl, just until combined and a ball of dough forms. (Dough should be sticky and slightly clumpy.)
3. Turn out dough onto a lightly floured surface. Using floured hands, gently shape into a round. Turn dough over, and tuck and rotate dough until edges are rounded and even. Transfer to a sheet of parchment paper, and pat into a 1½-inch-thick disk. Using a knife dipped in flour, cut a 1-inch-deep "X" across top of dough. Using tip of knife, prick a hole into each of the four sections of dough. Sprinkle remaining ⅓ cup (38 grams) cheese on top. Transfer on parchment paper to a baking sheet.
4. Bake for 15 minutes. Reduce oven temperature to 400°F (200°C), and bake until golden brown and an instant-read thermometer inserted in a section of bread registers 200°F (93°C), 15 to 20 minutes more. (If you tap bottom of loaf, it should sound hollow.) Remove from pan, and place on a wire rack. Let cool enough to handle, about 30 minutes. Best served warm.

PRO TIP: Perfectly baked soda bread doesn't just have a golden look and tender texture—it makes a lovely hollow sound when knocked with a knuckle. Give the bottom a tap to hear the echo of a well-baked loaf.

BISCUITS and SCONES

Three styles of biscuits and sweet and savory scones for any time of day highlight the diversity of these similar yet distinctly different breads

My Ultimate Buttermilk Biscuits

Makes about 12 biscuits

Though I was born and raised in Birmingham, Alabama, I consider myself a citizen of the world. My former career as a flight attendant allowed me to travel the world in search of the best baked goods. And although I've fallen in love with specialties from around the globe, my first baking love is good, old-fashioned Southern biscuits.

3½ cups (438 grams) White Lily® All-Purpose Flour (see Notes)
2 tablespoons (24 grams) granulated sugar
1 tablespoon (9 grams) kosher salt
1 tablespoon (15 grams) baking powder
½ teaspoon baking soda
1¼ cups (284 grams) cold unsalted butter, cubed
1 cup (240 grams) cold buttermilk
1 large egg (50 grams), lightly beaten
Flaked sea salt, for sprinkling

1. Preheat oven to 425°F (220°C). Line a baking sheet with parchment paper.
2. In a large bowl, whisk together flour, sugar, kosher salt, baking powder, and baking soda. Using a pastry blender, cut in cold butter until mixture is crumbly. Stir in cold buttermilk until a shaggy dough forms.
3. Turn out dough onto a lightly floured surface. Pat dough into a rectangle, and cut into fourths. Stack each fourth on top of each other, and pat down into a rectangle again. Repeat procedure three more times. Pat or roll dough to a 1-inch thickness. Using a 2½-inch round cutter dipped in flour, cut dough without twisting cutter, rerolling scraps as necessary. Place biscuits 2 inches apart on prepared pan. Freeze until cold, about 10 minutes.
4. Brush with egg wash, and sprinkle with sea salt.
5. Bake until golden brown, about 15 minutes. Serve warm.

Notes: *White Lily® is a finely milled soft winter wheat flour that is very popular throughout the Southern US but can be hard to find elsewhere. Visit* whitelily.com *for a store locator to find this flour in your area or to order online.*

You can also make your own White Lily-style flour blend for this recipe, which mimics the characteristics of the actual product. In a large bowl, whisk together 1¾ cups (219 grams) all-purpose flour and 1¾ cups plus 1½ tablespoons (221 grams) sifted bleached cake flour. Be sure to sift the cake flour before you measure it.

Buttermilk Biscuits 101

Great biscuits depend on cold butter and gentle handling. As the biscuits bake, small pieces of butter melt and release steam, lifting the dough and creating the tender, flaky layers that define a good biscuit. Overworking the dough develops gluten and leads to tough biscuits, so mix just until the dough comes together.

European-style butter softens quickly because of its higher fat content. If your kitchen is warm, freezing the butter before cutting it into the flour helps keep the pieces firm. Those small pieces of butter create the steam pockets that give biscuits their lift.

Cut the butter into the flour mixture until the pieces are about pea-size. Pieces that are too large can smear into the dough, while pieces that are too small won't create distinct layers.

Once the buttermilk is added, stir just until a shaggy dough forms. Turn the dough onto a lightly floured surface and gently pat it into a rectangle. The folding process creates the biscuit's signature layers: Cut the dough into sections, stack them, and pat the dough out again. Repeating this step several times builds flakiness without overworking the dough.

Press or roll the dough to about a 1-inch thickness. Using a floured 2½-inch round cutter, cut straight down without twisting. Twisting seals the edges and can prevent biscuits from rising fully. Chill the shaped biscuits briefly before baking so the butter stays cold until the biscuits hit the oven. That temperature contrast creates the steam that lifts and separates the layers.

Brush the tops with egg wash and sprinkle with flaked sea salt. Bake until golden brown and the biscuits are tall and flaky. Serve warm.

Drop Biscuits

Makes 11 biscuits

This recipe is a breezy wonder, with craggy, peaked tops that offer a bit of crunch over a soft interior. A final brush of melted butter gives the tops a soft sheen.

½ cup (113 grams) cold unsalted butter, cubed
1¾ cups (219 grams) all-purpose flour
1½ cups (188 grams) bleached cake flour
2 tablespoons (24 grams) granulated sugar
1 tablespoon (15 grams) baking powder
1 teaspoon kosher salt
1¾ cups (420 grams) cold buttermilk
Melted butter, for brushing

1. Freeze cold butter for 10 to 15 minutes.
2. Preheat oven to 400°F (200°C). Line a baking sheet with parchment paper.
3. In a large bowl, whisk together flours, sugar, baking powder, and salt. Using a pastry blender, cut in cold butter until mixture is crumbly and butter is the size of peas. Stir in cold buttermilk just until combined. (Dough will be sticky and wet.)
4. Using a ¼-cup spring-loaded scoop, scoop dough (about 86 grams), and drop 2 inches apart onto prepared pan. Brush melted butter onto dough.
5. Bake for 8 minutes. Reduce oven temperature to 375°F (190°C), and bake until golden brown, 8 to 10 minutes more. Best served hot. Store in an airtight container for up to 3 days.

Angel Biscuits

Makes 16 to 18 biscuits

Supremely light and fluffy, these biscuits use three leavening agents—yeast, baking powder, and baking soda—to achieve their heavenly texture. Best described as a mix between a flaky biscuit and a soft yeast roll, angel biscuits are as simple as they are delicious.

---

1 cup (227 grams) cold unsalted butter, cubed
2 cups (480 grams) warm buttermilk (110°F/43°C to 115°F/46°C)
2¼ teaspoons (7 grams) instant yeast
6 cups (750 grams) all-purpose flour, divided
¼ cup (50 grams) granulated sugar
5 teaspoons (15 grams) kosher salt
1 tablespoon (15 grams) baking powder
½ teaspoon baking soda
Melted butter

1. Freeze cold butter for about 10 minutes.
2. In a medium bowl, whisk together warm buttermilk and yeast until yeast dissolves. Let stand until foamy, 5 to 10 minutes.
3. Preheat oven to 425°F (220°C). Line a rimmed baking sheet with parchment paper.
4. In a large bowl, combine 3 cups (375 grams) flour and sugar. Add yeast mixture, and stir until just combined. Let stand for 3 to 5 minutes.
5. In another medium bowl, whisk together salt, baking powder, baking soda, and remaining 3 cups (375 grams) flour. Add cold butter, tossing to coat. Using a pastry blender or 2 forks, cut in cold butter until pieces are smaller than peas and mixture is crumbly. Add butter mixture to flour-yeast mixture. Using your hand, knead dough in bowl until dough just comes together.
6. Turn out dough onto a lightly floured surface. Press or roll into a 1-inch-thick disk. Fold dough in half, and press or roll into a 1-inch-thick disk. Using a 2½-inch round cutter dipped in flour, cut dough without twisting cutter, and place about 1½ inches apart on prepared pan. (See Note.) Reroll scraps once by pushing scraps together, folding in half, and then pressing or rolling to a 1-inch thickness. Discard remaining scraps. Cover and let rise in a warm, draft-free place (75°F/24°C) until puffed, about 15 minutes.
7. Brush biscuits with melted butter.
8. Bake until golden brown, 10 to 14 minutes. Brush again with melted butter; serve warm.

Note: *Biscuits can be baked touching if you want a softer biscuit. If you like biscuits with crispy edges, bake about 1½ inches apart. Biscuits that are touching will take longer to bake, and biscuits with space between them will bake faster.*

Gruyère, Onion, and Pepper Biscuits

Makes 16 biscuits

The secret to these savory biscuits is cold ingredients and a quick layering process. Once formed, the shaggy dough is swiftly quartered and stacked, creating unmistakable layers that lead to tall and flaky biscuits that are great on their own or served with soups, salads, and even as the base of a hearty breakfast sandwich.

---

4 cups (500 grams) all-purpose flour
2 tablespoons (24 grams) granulated sugar
1½ tablespoons (23 grams) baking powder
4 teaspoons (12 grams) kosher salt
1 tablespoon (8 grams) dried minced onion
1½ teaspoons (3 grams) ground black pepper
¼ teaspoon baking soda
1 cup (227 grams) cold unsalted butter, cubed
1⅓ cups (151 grams) shredded Gruyère cheese, divided
1½ cups (360 grams) cold buttermilk
1 tablespoon (14 grams) unsalted butter, melted

1. Preheat oven to 425°F (220°C). Line a baking sheet with parchment paper.
2. In a large bowl, whisk together flour, sugar, baking powder, salt, onion, pepper, and baking soda. Add cold butter, and toss to coat. Using a pastry blender or 2 forks, cut in butter until mixture is crumbly and butter pieces are pea-size. Stir in 1 cup (113 grams) cheese. Add cold buttermilk, and stir with a fork until a shaggy dough forms.
3. Turn out dough onto a lightly floured surface, and pat into a 9-inch square (about 1 inch thick). (Dough will be crumbly.) Using a bench scraper, cut dough in fourths. Stack fourths, and pat or roll into a 9-inch square. Repeat procedure two more times. Using a knife or bench scraper dipped in flour, cut dough into 16 (2¼-inch) squares. Place at least ½ inch apart on prepared pan. Freeze for 15 minutes.
4. Brush top of dough with melted butter, and sprinkle with remaining ⅓ cup (38 grams) cheese.
5. Bake until golden brown, 16 to 18 minutes. Best served warm. Store in an airtight container for up to 3 days.

Stuffing Biscuits

Makes 12 biscuits

The blend of savory herbs, spices, and comforting aromatics that you know and love in traditional Thanksgiving stuffing (or dressing!) is made over into these tender and flaky biscuits. This creative twist on a holiday classic not only embodies the essential flavors of this special day but is also perfect for building an epic leftover turkey sandwich.

---

2 tablespoons (28 grams) unsalted butter
¾ cup (86 grams) finely diced celery
⅓ cup (37 grams) finely diced sweet onion
4 cups (500 grams) all-purpose flour
4 teaspoons (20 grams) baking powder
1 tablespoon (9 grams) kosher salt
1 tablespoon (12 grams) granulated sugar
1½ teaspoons (3 grams) poultry seasoning
½ teaspoon garlic powder
½ teaspoon ground black pepper
1 cup (227 grams) cold unsalted butter, cubed
½ cup (57 grams) shredded Gruyère cheese
1¼ cups (300 grams) cold buttermilk
1 large egg (50 grams)
1 tablespoon (15 grams) water
Flaked sea salt

1. Line a rimmed baking sheet with parchment paper.
2. In a medium skillet, melt butter over medium-high heat. Add celery and onion; cook, stirring frequently, until tender and fragrant, 5 to 6 minutes. Remove from heat; let cool completely.
3. In a large bowl, whisk together flour, baking powder, kosher salt, sugar, poultry seasoning, garlic powder, and pepper. Add cold butter, tossing to coat. Using a pastry blender or your hands, cut in butter until mixture is crumbly and butter pieces are pea-size. Stir in cooled vegetable mixture and cheese. Add cold buttermilk; stir with a fork until a shaggy dough forms. (Do not overmix.)
4. Turn out dough onto a lightly floured surface. (Dough will be crumbly and almost dry.) Pat dough into a square about 1¼ inches thick. Using a bench scraper or sharp knife, cut into fourths. Stack fourths on top of each other, and pat to a 1¼-inch thickness. Repeat procedure three more times. (Dough may seem too shaggy at first but will come together and be easier to work with as you go.)
5. Roll dough into a 1¼-inch-thick square. Using a 2¼-inch round cutter dipped in flour, cut 12 rounds from dough, rerolling scraps once. Place 1 inch apart on prepared pan. Freeze for 15 minutes.
6. Preheat oven to 425°F (220°C).
7. In a small bowl, whisk together egg and 1 tablespoon (15 grams) water; brush onto biscuits. Sprinkle with sea salt.
8. Bake until golden brown, 18 to 22 minutes. Let cool on pan for 5 minutes. Best served warm. Store in an airtight container for up to 3 days.

PRO TIP: Biscuits can be prepared through step 5, frozen until firm, and then transferred to a heavy-duty resealable bag to freeze for up to 1 month. Bake as directed from frozen, adding about 5 minutes to bake time.

Browned Butter Sweet Potato Biscuits

Makes 15 biscuits

Using buttermilk in your biscuits helps the dough rise and creates taller, fluffier biscuits. The subtle tang from the buttermilk pairs beautifully with the browned butter, sage, and sweet potato for a harmony of flavors perfect for fall.

1¼ cups (284 grams) unsalted butter
1 tablespoon (4 grams) packed fresh sage leaves
3¼ cups (406 grams) all-purpose flour
1 cup (220 grams) cold mashed baked sweet potato
2 tablespoons (24 grams) granulated sugar
1 tablespoon (15 grams) baking powder
1 tablespoon (9 grams) kosher salt
½ teaspoon baking soda
½ cup (120 grams) cold buttermilk
1 large egg (50 grams)
1 tablespoon (15 grams) water
Flaked sea salt
Softened butter, to serve

1. In a light-colored medium saucepan, melt butter over medium heat. Add sage; cook, stirring frequently, until butter is fragrant and a deep amber color, 8 to 10 minutes. Pour into a shallow baking dish, and let cool for 10 to 15 minutes. Freeze until solid, about 30 minutes.
2. Preheat oven to 400°F (200°C). Line 2 baking sheets with parchment paper.
3. In the work bowl of a food processor, pulse flour, cold sweet potato, sugar, baking powder, salt, and baking soda until combined.
4. Cut frozen butter into 1-inch pieces; add to flour mixture, and pulse just until butter pieces are the size of small peas and mixture is crumbly. Add cold buttermilk, and pulse until a shaggy dough forms.
5. Turn out dough onto a lightly floured surface. Pat dough into a rectangle about 1 inch thick. Cut dough into fourths. Stack fourths on top of each other, and pat into a rectangle. Repeat procedure three more times.
6. Pat or roll dough to a ¾-inch thickness. Using a 2½-inch round cutter dipped in flour, cut dough without twisting cutter, rerolling scraps as necessary. (To reroll scraps, stack pieces on top of each other, and pat to a ¾-inch thickness.) Place 2 inches apart on prepared pan. Freeze until cold, about 10 minutes.
7. In a small bowl, whisk together egg and 1 tablespoon (15 grams) water; brush onto biscuits, and sprinkle with sea salt.
8. Bake until golden brown, 15 to 18 minutes, covering with foil after 10 minutes of baking to prevent excess browning. Serve with softened butter.

Hummingbird Scones

Makes 4 scones

As simple as they are delicious, these Southern classic-inspired scones include every flavor of the beloved cake but in quick bread form. Bursting with fruity banana, lightly tangy pineapple, and crunchy toasted pecans, these scones balance perfectly between decadence and light, fresh flavors. Topped with a smooth cream cheese glaze, it'll almost be like eating cake for breakfast, minus the hassle.

1¾ cups (219 grams) all-purpose flour
3 tablespoons (36 grams) granulated sugar
1 teaspoon ground cinnamon
¾ teaspoon kosher salt
½ teaspoon baking powder
¼ teaspoon baking soda
6 tablespoons (84 grams) cold unsalted butter, cubed
¼ cup (60 grams) cold buttermilk
1 teaspoon vanilla extract
½ cup (114 grams) mashed ripe banana (about 1 medium banana)
¼ cup (67 grams) pressed drained crushed pineapple
½ cup (57 grams) chopped pecans, toasted
Vanilla Cream Cheese Glaze (recipe follows)
Garnish: chopped toasted pecans

1. Preheat oven to 375°F (190°C). Line a baking sheet with parchment paper.
2. In a large bowl, whisk together flour, sugar, cinnamon, salt, baking powder, and baking soda. Using your hands or a pastry blender, cut in cold butter until mixture resembles coarse crumbs. Make a well in center.
3. In a medium bowl, whisk together cold buttermilk and vanilla. Add banana and pineapple. Add buttermilk mixture and pecans to flour mixture, and stir with a spatula until dry ingredients are fully moistened. Knead with your hands once or twice just until dough is smooth and fully hydrated.
4. Turn out dough, and pat into a 6-inch circle. Cut into fourths. Place on prepared pan.
5. Bake until golden and an instant-read thermometer inserted in center registers 205°F (96°C), 25 to 30 minutes. Let cool on pan for 10 minutes. Remove from pan, and let cool completely on a wire rack.
6. Spread Vanilla Cream Cheese Glaze onto cooled scones, and garnish with pecans, if desired. Store in an airtight container for up to 3 days.

Vanilla Cream Cheese Glaze

Makes about ¾ cup

4 ounces (113 grams) cream cheese, softened
¼ cup (30 grams) confectioners' sugar
2 tablespoons (30 grams) whole milk
1 teaspoon vanilla extract

1. In a small bowl, whisk together all ingredients until smooth and spreadable.

Spiced Apple Scones

Makes 8 scones

Fragrant and not too sweet, these scones are best paired with a cup of coffee or tea for an afternoon snack.

---

2 cups (250 grams) all-purpose flour
¼ cup (50 grams) granulated sugar
2½ teaspoons (13 grams) baking powder
1½ teaspoons (3 grams) Chinese five-spice powder, divided
1 teaspoon kosher salt
¼ teaspoon baking soda
6 tablespoons (84 grams) cold unsalted butter, cubed
1 cup (120 grams) finely diced firm sweet apple
1 cup (240 grams) plus 8 tablespoons (120 grams) cold heavy whipping cream, divided
1½ teaspoons vanilla bean paste, divided
1 cup (120 grams) confectioners' sugar

1. Preheat oven to 375°F (190°C). Line a rimmed baking sheet with parchment paper.
2. In a large bowl, whisk together flour, granulated sugar, baking powder, 1¼ teaspoons (3 grams) five-spice powder, salt, and baking soda. Using a pastry blender or 2 forks, cut in cold butter until mixture resembles coarse crumbs. Stir in apple.
3. In a small bowl, stir together 1 cup (240 grams) cold cream and 1 teaspoon vanilla bean paste. Add cream mixture to flour mixture, and stir until combined and no dry streaks remain.
4. Turn out dough onto a lightly floured surface. Gently knead two to three times to bring dough together. Roll or pat dough into a 7-inch circle (about 1 inch thick). Using a floured knife or bench scraper, cut into 8 wedges. Place at least 2 inches apart on prepared pan. Freeze until firm, about 15 minutes.
5. Brush 2 tablespoons (30 grams) cold cream onto dough.
6. Bake until golden brown and a wooden pick inserted in center comes out clean, 15 to 20 minutes. Let cool on pan for 10 minutes. Remove from pan, and let cool completely on a wire rack.
7. In a medium bowl, whisk together confectioners' sugar, 5 tablespoons (75 grams) cold cream, remaining ½ teaspoon vanilla paste, and remaining ¼ teaspoon five-spice powder until smooth and pourable; whisk in up to remaining 1 tablespoon (15 grams) cold cream if needed. Drizzle glaze onto cooled scones. Store in an airtight container for up to 3 days.

Dill, Sour Cream, and Potato Scones

Makes 10 scones

These delicious scones boast an irresistibly fluffy texture thanks to the addition of mashed potatoes. Sour cream lends a subtle tang and richness, and fresh dill brightens the dough with a sweet, almost lemony flavor.

---

3 cups (375 grams) all-purpose flour
2 tablespoons (8 grams) chopped fresh dill
4 teaspoons (20 grams) baking powder
2 teaspoons (8 grams) granulated sugar
1½ teaspoons (5 grams) kosher salt
½ teaspoon ground black pepper
½ cup (113 grams) cold unsalted butter, cubed
1 cup (232 grams) plain mashed russet potatoes, room temperature
⅔ cup (160 grams) cold sour cream
½ cup (120 grams) ice water
1 large egg (50 grams), lightly beaten
Sour cream and fresh dill, to serve

1. Preheat oven to 400°F (200°C). Line a baking sheet with parchment paper.
2. In a large bowl, whisk together flour, dill, baking powder, sugar, salt, and pepper. Using a pastry blender or 2 forks, cut in cold butter until mixture is crumbly.
3. In a small bowl, whisk together potatoes, cold sour cream, and ½ cup (120 grams) ice water. Add potato mixture to flour mixture, stirring with a fork just until mixture starts to come together. Using your hands, knead dough just until combined.
4. Turn out dough onto a lightly floured surface, and roll to a 1-inch thickness. Using a 2½-inch round cutter dipped in flour, cut dough without twisting cutter, rerolling scraps once, and place at least 1 inch apart on prepared pan. Brush top of scones with egg.
5. Bake until golden brown, 20 to 25 minutes. Let cool on pan for 5 minutes. Serve warm with sour cream and dill.

Maple Oat Scones

Makes 9 scones

These maple-scented scones are loaded with chewy oats for a hearty breakfast on the go or a special weekend brunch sweet treat.

3 cups (375 grams) all-purpose flour
½ cup (40 grams) old-fashioned oats
¼ cup (55 grams) firmly packed dark brown sugar
1 tablespoon (15 grams) baking powder
2½ teaspoons (6 grams) kosher salt, divided
¾ cup (170 grams) cold unsalted butter, cubed
1 cup (240 grams) plus 3 tablespoons (45 grams) cold buttermilk, divided
1 teaspoon maple extract
1 cup (120 grams) confectioners' sugar
2 tablespoons (14 grams) maple syrup
Garnish: toasted old-fashioned oats

1. Preheat oven to 375°F (190°C). Line a baking sheet with parchment paper.
2. In a large bowl, whisk together flour, oats, brown sugar, baking powder, and 2 teaspoons (6 grams) salt. Using a pastry blender or 2 forks, cut in cold butter until mixture resembles coarse crumbs.
3. In a small bowl, stir together 1 cup (240 grams) cold buttermilk and maple extract. Gradually add buttermilk mixture to flour mixture, stirring with a fork just until dry ingredients are moistened.
4. Turn out dough onto a clean surface; gently knead until dough comes together, 8 to 10 times. On a very lightly floured surface, roll dough into a 7-inch circle (about 1 inch thick). Using a 2½-inch round cutter dipped in flour, cut dough without twisting cutter, rerolling scraps as necessary. Place 2 inches apart on prepared pan. Freeze for 15 minutes.
5. Bake until light golden brown and a wooden pick inserted in center comes out clean, 15 to 20 minutes. Let cool on pan for 5 minutes.
6. In a small bowl, whisk together confectioners' sugar, maple syrup, remaining 3 tablespoons (45 grams) cold buttermilk, and remaining ½ teaspoon salt until smooth. Just before serving, dip top of scones in glaze. Garnish with toasted oats, if desired. Store in an airtight container for up to 4 days.

FILLED, STUFFED, and TOPPED

Whether spiraled with meat and cheese, glazed with crunchy nuts, or studded with sweet fruit, these breads are bursting with diversely delicious flavors

My Favorite Cinnamon Rolls

Makes 9 rolls

I've found the secret to sweet roll perfection. Prior to baking, the rolls are doused with warm heavy cream, creating the dreamiest, most luscious cinnamon rolls you will ever sink your teeth into. Top them with a silky cream cheese icing for instant cinnamon roll bliss.

Dough:
- 1 cup (240 grams) warm whole milk (105°F/41°C to 110°F /43°C), divided
- 2¼ teaspoons (7 grams) active dry yeast
- ⅓ cup (76 grams) unsalted butter, melted
- ⅓ cup (67 grams) granulated sugar
- ¼ cup (60 grams) sour cream, room temperature
- 1 large egg (50 grams), lightly beaten and room temperature
- 4 cups (500 grams) all-purpose flour, divided
- 1 teaspoon (3 grams) kosher salt

Filling:
- ¾ cup (165 grams) firmly packed light brown sugar
- ½ cup plus 2 tablespoons (141 grams) unsalted butter, softened
- 1 tablespoon plus 1 teaspoon (8 grams) ground cinnamon

- ½ cup (120 grams) warm heavy whipping cream (105°F/41°C to 110°F/43°C)

Icing:
- ½ cup (112 grams) cream cheese, softened
- 1½ tablespoons (21 grams) unsalted butter, softened
- 1½ cups (180 grams) confectioners' sugar
- 1 tablespoon (15 grams) whole milk, room temperature

1. For dough: In a medium bowl, combine ¾ cup (180 grams) warm milk and yeast. Let stand until foamy, about 10 minutes.
2. In the bowl of a stand mixer fitted with the paddle attachment, beat melted butter, granulated sugar, sour cream, egg, and remaining ¼ cup (60 grams) warm milk at low speed just until combined.
3. In a large bowl, whisk together 3⅔ cups (458 grams) flour and salt. Stir half of flour mixture into butter mixture. With mixer on low speed, add yeast mixture, beating just until combined. Beat in remaining flour mixture.
4. Switch to the dough hook attachment. Beat at medium speed until smooth and elastic, 4 to 8 minutes; add up to remaining ⅓ cup (42 grams) flour, 1 tablespoon (8 grams) at a time, if needed. (Dough should pass the windowpane test; see page 16.) Shape dough into a smooth ball.
5. Spray a large bowl with cooking spray. Place dough in bowl, turning to grease top. Loosely cover and let rise in a warm, draft-free place (75°F/24°C) until doubled in size, about 1 hour.
6. Lightly punch down dough. Cover and let stand for 5 minutes.
7. For filling: In a medium bowl, stir together brown sugar, butter, and cinnamon.
8. Spray a 9-inch square baking pan with baking spray with flour.
9. On a lightly floured surface, roll dough into an 18x16-inch rectangle. Spread filling onto dough, leaving a ¾-inch border on one long side. Starting with long side opposite border, roll up dough into a log, pinching seam to seal. Gently stretch dough log to 19 inches long.
10. Trim ½ inch off each end of log. Using unflavored dental floss, score top of dough into 9 (2-inch-wide) pieces; place floss under log, lining up with scores, and bring ends of floss together quickly to create an even cut. (Alternatively, slice log with a sharp serrated knife.) Press up center of rolls on underside, and place rolls, cut side up, in prepared pan. Let rise in a warm, draft-free place (75°F/24°C) until puffed and rolls are touching, 30 to 45 minutes.
11. Place a piece of foil on bottom rack of oven. Preheat oven to 350°F (180°C).
12. Drizzle warm cream all over rolls in pan.
13. Bake until golden brown and an instant-read thermometer inserted in center registers 190°F (88°C), 30 to 35 minutes. Let cool for 10 minutes.
14. For icing: In the bowl of a stand mixer fitted with the paddle attachment, beat cream cheese and butter at medium speed until creamy, 4 to 5 minutes. With mixer on low speed, gradually add confectioners' sugar, beating until fluffy. Beat in milk until combined. Spread icing onto warm rolls. Best served warm. Cover and refrigerate for up to 3 days.

Cinnamon Roll 101

Great cinnamon rolls begin with a soft, well-developed dough and careful shaping.

After the dough has risen, turn it out onto a lightly floured surface and roll it into a large rectangle. Aim for a consistent thickness so the rolls bake evenly.

Spread the softened filling evenly over the surface, leaving a small border along one long edge to help seal the roll.

Starting with one long side, roll up the dough into a tight log. Keeping the roll snug helps create defined spirals.

For clean slices, cut the log into even portions using a sharp knife or unflavored dental floss. Dental floss works especially well because it cuts through the dough without compressing the layers.

Arrange the rolls in a greased baking pan, leaving a little space between each roll so they can expand during the final rise. Let the rolls proof until they are puffy and touching.

Just before baking, pour warm cream over the risen rolls. The cream helps the rolls stay soft and tender.

Bake until the rolls are golden brown and set in the centers. Let cool slightly before topping with cream cheese icing so it melts gently into the spirals.

Mexican Chocolate Cinnamon Rolls

Makes 12 rolls

I filled these golden rolls with chocolate, but not just any chocolate—Mexican cinnamon chocolate. Stone-ground, Mexican-style dark chocolate is infused with warm cinnamon and has a subtle grittiness that gives these sweet rolls even more explosive flavor and complex texture. Once you smother the rolls in the luscious Cream Cheese Glaze, serve them straight from the skillet to keep them warm and gooey.

3½ to 3¾ cups (438 to 469 grams) all-purpose flour, divided
½ cup (100 grams) granulated sugar, divided
2¼ teaspoons (7 grams) active dry yeast
2 teaspoons (5 grams) kosher salt, divided
½ cup (120 grams) water
½ cup (120 grams) whole milk
⅔ cup (152 grams) unsalted butter, softened and divided
1 large egg (50 grams), room temperature
2 tablespoons (10 grams) Dutch process cocoa powder
½ teaspoon ground cinnamon
⅔ cup (113 grams) chopped Mexican-style stone-ground cinnamon chocolate (3 disks) (see Pro Tip on opposite page)
Cream Cheese Glaze (recipe follows)

1. In the bowl of a stand mixer fitted with the paddle attachment, combine 1½ cups (188 grams) flour, ¼ cup (50 grams) sugar, yeast, and 1½ teaspoons (5 grams) salt.
2. In a medium saucepan, heat ½ cup (120 grams) water, milk, and ⅓ cup (76 grams) butter over medium heat until an instant-read thermometer registers 120°F (49°C) to 130°F (54°C). Add hot milk mixture to flour mixture, and beat at medium speed until combined. Add egg, beating until combined. With mixer on low speed, gradually add 2 cups (250 grams) flour, beating just until combined and stopping to scrape sides of bowl.
3. Switch to the dough hook attachment. Beat at low speed until a soft, smooth, and somewhat sticky dough forms and pulls away from sides of bowl, 8 to 9 minutes; add up to remaining ¼ cup (31 grams) flour, if necessary. Turn out onto a lightly floured surface, and shape into a smooth round.
4. Lightly spray a large bowl. Place dough in bowl, turning to grease top. Cover and let rise in a warm, draft-free place (75°F/24°C) until doubled in size, 40 minutes to 1 hour.
5. Spray a 10-inch cast-iron skillet with cooking spray.
6. In a small bowl, whisk together cocoa, cinnamon, remaining ⅓ cup (76 grams) butter, remaining ¼ cup (50 grams) sugar, and remaining ½ teaspoon salt.
7. Lightly punch down dough. Cover and let stand for 5 minutes. Turn out dough onto a lightly floured surface, and roll into an 18x12-inch rectangle. Spread cocoa mixture onto dough, leaving a ½-inch border on one long side. Sprinkle chopped chocolate onto cocoa mixture. Starting with long side opposite border, roll up dough into a log; pinch seam to seal. Gently shape log to 18 inches long and even thickness, if necessary. Using a serrated knife dipped in flour, cut log into 12 slices (about 1½ inches thick). Place slices, cut side down, in prepared skillet. Cover and let rise in a warm, draft-free place (75°F/24°C) until puffed, 20 to 30 minutes.
8. Preheat oven to 350°F (180°C).
9. Bake until light golden brown and an instant-read thermometer inserted in center registers 190°F (88°C), 35 to 40 minutes, loosely covering with foil to prevent excess browning, if necessary. Let cool in skillet for 10 minutes. Top with Cream Cheese Glaze. Serve warm or at room temperature.

Cream Cheese Glaze

Makes about ¾ cup

4 ounces (113 grams) cream cheese, softened
1½ tablespoons (11 grams) confectioners' sugar
2 to 3 tablespoons (30 to 45 grams) whole milk

1. In a medium bowl, whisk cream cheese until smooth. Whisk in confectioners' sugar. Whisk in milk, 1 tablespoon (15 grams) at a time, until fluid.

PRO TIP: I used Taza Chocolate Cinnamon Dark Chocolate Mexicano, available at Whole Foods, local Hispanic grocery stores, or online. Very minimally processed, Mexican chocolate has a grainier, chalkier texture than the chocolate you might normally get and offers more-complex, explosive flavor. Any type of Mexican cinnamon dark chocolate, available at most grocery stores, or 50% cacao dark chocolate will work in this recipe.

Pecan-Maple-Bourbon Sticky Buns

Makes 12 buns

Crunchy pecans are the perfect addition to these pillow-soft swirls, and your home will be filled with a buttery, spiced, mouthwatering aroma while they bake!

Dough:
1 cup (240 grams) warm whole milk (110°F/43°C to 115°F/46°C)
5 tablespoons (60 grams) granulated sugar, divided
2¼ teaspoons (7 grams) active dry yeast
3¾ cups (468 grams) all-purpose flour
1 tablespoon (9 grams) kosher salt
2 large eggs (100 grams), room temperature
2 teaspoons (8 grams) vanilla extract
½ cup (113 grams) unsalted butter, cubed and room temperature

Topping:
½ cup (110 grams) firmly packed light brown sugar
½ cup (170 grams) maple syrup
6 tablespoons (84 grams) unsalted butter
5 tablespoons (75 grams) bourbon
½ teaspoon kosher salt
1 cup (100 grams) pecan halves
½ cup (57 grams) chopped pecans

Filling:
⅔ cup (147 grams) firmly packed light brown sugar
½ cup (113 grams) unsalted butter, room temperature
1 tablespoon (6 grams) ground cinnamon
½ teaspoon kosher salt
1 cup (113 grams) finely chopped pecans

1. For dough: In a small bowl, stir together warm milk, 1 tablespoon (12 grams) granulated sugar, and yeast. Let stand until foamy, about 5 minutes.
2. In the bowl of a stand mixer, whisk together 2 cups (250 grams) flour, salt, and remaining 4 tablespoons (48 grams) granulated sugar. Add yeast mixture, eggs, and vanilla; using the paddle attachment, beat at low speed until combined, about 1 minute. Scrape sides of bowl. With mixer on low speed, gradually add remaining 1¾ cups (219 grams) flour, beating until a shaggy dough forms; scrape sides of bowl.
3. Switch to the dough hook attachment. Beat at medium-low speed until dough is smooth, elastic, and slightly tacky, 7 to 9 minutes. With mixer on medium-low speed, add butter, 1 tablespoon (14 grams) at a time, beating until combined after each addition (about 8 minutes total). Beat until a smooth, elastic dough forms, 6 to 8 minutes. (Dough will be tacky but should clean sides of the bowl.) Turn out dough onto a very lightly floured surface, and knead 5 to 8 times. Shape dough into a smooth round.
4. Lightly oil a large bowl. Place dough in bowl, turning to grease top. Cover and let rise in a warm, draft-free place (75°F/24°C) until doubled in size, 45 minutes to 1 hour. (Alternatively, cover and refrigerate overnight; punch down dough, and let stand at room temperature for 30 minutes before shaping.)
5. Lightly spray a 13x9-inch baking dish with baking spray with flour.
6. For topping: In a medium saucepan, bring brown sugar, maple syrup, butter, bourbon, and salt to a boil over medium-high heat, stirring occasionally until sugar dissolves. Cook, stirring frequently, until slightly thickened, 4 to 5 minutes. Pour mixture into prepared pan, lightly spreading to edges. Sprinkle pecan halves and chopped pecans on top.
7. For filling: In another small bowl, stir together brown sugar, butter, cinnamon, and salt.
8. Punch down dough. Cover and let stand for 5 minutes. Turn out dough onto a lightly floured surface, and roll into an 18x12-inch rectangle. Spread filling mixture onto dough, leaving a ¼-inch border on one long side. Sprinkle finely chopped pecans on top. Starting with long side opposite border, roll up dough into a log. Cut into 12 slices (about 1½ inches each). Place on top of pecans in prepared pan. Cover and let rise in a warm, draft-free place (75°F/24°C) until doubled in size, 45 minutes to 1 hour.
9. Preheat oven to 350°F (180°C).
10. Bake until golden brown, 35 to 40 minutes. Let cool for 5 minutes. Invert buns onto a rimmed serving dish. Serve warm or at room temperature. Store in an airtight container for up to 3 days.

Cranberry-Orange Crescent Rolls

Makes 24 rolls

Buttery and rich, these rolls are filled with dried sweetened cranberries, orange zest, and a touch of vanilla and baked to golden perfection. Whether you serve them alongside something sweet or savory, this recipe makes a batch big enough to share all the holiday cheer.

4¼ to 4½ cups (531 to 562 grams) all-purpose flour, divided
1½ tablespoons (14 grams) instant yeast
3½ teaspoons (11 grams) kosher salt
¾ cup (180 grams) whole milk
½ cup (113 grams) unsalted butter
¼ cup (60 grams) water
2 tablespoons (24 grams) granulated sugar
3 tablespoons (63 grams) clover honey, divided
2 teaspoons (5 grams) tightly packed orange zest
¾ cup (112 grams) lightly packed sweetened dried cranberries, chopped
1 large egg (50 grams), room temperature
1 large egg yolk (19 grams), room temperature
1 teaspoon vanilla extract
4 tablespoons (56 grams) unsalted butter, melted and divided

1. In the bowl of a stand mixer, whisk together 1 cup (125 grams) flour, yeast, and salt by hand.
2. In a small saucepan, heat milk, butter, ¼ cup (60 grams) water, sugar, 2 tablespoons (42 grams) honey, and orange zest over medium-low heat until an instant-read thermometer registers 120°F (49°C) to 130°F (54°C). Add hot milk mixture to flour mixture; using the paddle attachment, beat at medium-low speed just until combined, 1 to 2 minutes, stopping to scrape sides of bowl. Add cranberries, egg, egg yolk, and vanilla; beat at low speed until combined. With mixer on low speed, gradually add 3¼ cups (406 grams) flour, beating until combined.
3. Switch to the dough hook attachment. Beat at low speed until a soft, somewhat sticky, and elastic dough forms, 6 to 9 minutes; add up to remaining ¼ cup (31 grams) flour, 1 tablespoon (8 grams) at a time, if dough is too sticky. (Dough may still stick to sides and bottom of bowl but should pass the windowpane test; see page 16.) Turn out dough onto a lightly floured surface, and shape into a ball.
4. Spray a large bowl with cooking spray. Place dough in bowl, turning to grease top. Cover and let rise in a warm, draft-free place (75°F/24°C) until doubled in size, 30 to 45 minutes.
5. Line 2 baking sheets with parchment paper.
6. Punch down dough; cover and let stand for 10 minutes or refrigerate overnight. (If refrigerating overnight, punch down dough an additional 1 to 2 times during first hour of refrigeration.) On a lightly floured surface, divide dough in half (about 580 grams each). Gently shape each half into a round; cover and let stand for 15 minutes.
7. Roll half of dough into a 14-inch circle. (Keep remaining dough covered to prevent it from drying out.) Using a pastry wheel, cut dough into 12 triangles. Place dough triangles with smoothest side down; starting from base of each triangle, roll up dough, pressing pointed ends into rolls to seal. Place rolls, pointed end securely tucked under, 1½ to 2 inches apart on prepared pans. Repeat procedure with remaining dough. Cover and let rise in a warm, draft-free place (75°F/24°C) until doubled in size, 35 to 45 minutes.
8. Preheat oven to 350°F (180°C).
9. Brush 2 tablespoons (28 grams) melted butter onto dough.
10. Bake, one pan at a time, until golden brown, 10 to 14 minutes, rotating pan halfway through baking.
11. In a small bowl, whisk together remaining 2 tablespoons (28 grams) melted butter and remaining 1 tablespoon (21 grams) honey. Brush honey butter onto hot rolls. Let cool on pans for at least 30 minutes before serving. Best enjoyed same day but can be stored in a somewhat airtight container at room temperature for up to 2 days.

Note: *Be sure the pointed ends are significantly and securely tucked under your crescent rolls before the second rise and bake for best shape.*

Chocolate-Cherry Brioche Buns

Makes 20 buns

These buns procure their magical power from tangzhong, a paste or roux made from milk and flour. It has two essential purposes: lock in moisture while keeping your buns light and bouncy and keep the buns fresher for longer. With decadent chocolate and tart cherries folded into soft, buttery, rich brioche, these buns are both elegant and comforting.

Tangzhong:
6 tablespoons (90 grams) whole milk
3 tablespoons (24 grams) all-purpose flour

Dough:
2⅔ cups (333 grams) all-purpose flour
3 tablespoons (36 grams) granulated sugar
2¼ teaspoons (7 grams) instant yeast
2¼ teaspoons (7 grams) kosher salt
½ cup (120 grams) hot whole milk (120°F/49°C to 130°F/54°C)
2 large eggs (100 grams), room temperature
½ cup (113 grams) unsalted butter, cubed and room temperature
½ cup (85 grams) coarsely chopped 60% cacao bittersweet chocolate
½ cup (64 grams) finely chopped dried cherries

1 large egg (50 grams)
1 tablespoon (15 grams) water

1. For tangzhong: In a small saucepan, whisk together milk and flour; cook over medium-low heat, whisking constantly, until thickened, whisk leaves lines on bottom of pan, and an instant-read thermometer registers 150°F (66°C). (Mixture will look like mashed potatoes.)
2. Transfer to a small bowl, and let cool until an instant-read thermometer registers 130°F (54°C) or until room temperature.
3. For dough: In the bowl of a stand mixer, whisk together 1⅔ cups (208 grams) flour, sugar, yeast, and salt. Add cooled tangzhong, hot milk, and eggs; using the paddle attachment, beat at low speed until combined, about 1 minute. With mixer on low speed, gradually add remaining 1 cup (125 grams) flour, beating until a shaggy dough forms; scrape sides of bowl.
4. Switch to the dough hook attachment. Beat at medium-low speed until dough becomes smooth, elastic, and slightly tacky, 8 to 11 minutes. (Dough should pull away from sides of bowl.) With mixer on medium-low speed, add butter, 1 tablespoon (14 grams) at a time, beating until combined after each addition (7 to 8 minutes total). Increase mixer speed to medium, and beat until a smooth, elastic dough forms, about 10 minutes. Reduce mixer speed to low; add chocolate and cherries, beating until well combined.
5. Lightly oil a large bowl. Place dough in bowl, turning to grease top. Cover and let rise in a warm, draft-free place (75°F/24°C) until doubled in size, 1 to 1½ hours.
6. Line baking sheets with parchment paper.
7. Turn out dough onto a clean surface, and punch down dough. Press dough into a 10x8-inch rectangle. Divide dough into 20 portions (about 45 grams each). Using your hands, gently roll each portion into a smooth ball, lightly flouring hands as needed. Place 3 to 4 inches apart on prepared pans. Cover with lightly greased plastic wrap, and let rise in a warm, draft-free place (75°F/24°C) until doubled in size, about 1 hour.
8. Preheat oven to 375°F (190°C).
9. In another small bowl, whisk together egg and 1 tablespoon (15 grams) water; brush onto dough.
10. Bake until golden brown and an instant-read thermometer inserted in center registers 190°F (88°C), 8 to 10 minutes. Let cool on pans for 5 minutes. Remove from pans, and let cool completely on a wire rack. Store in an airtight container for up to 3 days.

Date-Pecan Bread

Makes 1 (9x5-inch) loaf

Enriching a bread dough with milk helps create a soft, tender crumb and adds a little sweetness. Dates' caramelly taste enhances the pecans in every bite of this soft loaf. Leftovers make fabulous French toast.

3½ cups (445 grams) bread flour
2 tablespoons (24 grams) granulated sugar
2¼ teaspoons (7 grams) instant yeast
1½ teaspoons (5 grams) kosher salt
1 cup (240 grams) hot whole milk (120°F/49°C to 130°F/54°C)
1 large egg (50 grams), room temperature
3 tablespoons (42 grams) unsalted butter, melted
2 tablespoons (42 grams) honey
1 cup (156 grams) whole pitted dates, chopped
¾ cup (85 grams) finely chopped toasted pecans
1 large egg white (30 grams), lightly beaten

1. In the bowl of a stand mixer fitted with the paddle attachment, beat flour, sugar, yeast, and salt at low speed until combined. Add hot milk; beat until a dough ball forms. Add egg, melted butter, and honey; beat until well combined.
2. Switch to the dough hook attachment. Beat at low speed until dough is smooth and elastic and passes the windowpane test (see page 16), 12 to 15 minutes. Add dates and pecans; beat until well combined.
3. Spray a large bowl with cooking spray. Place dough in bowl, turning to grease top. Cover and let rise in a warm, draft-free place (75°F/24°C) until doubled in size, 1 to 1½ hours.
4. Spray a 9x5-inch loaf pan with baking spray with flour. Line pan with parchment paper, letting excess extend over sides of pan.
5. Turn out dough onto a lightly floured surface. Gently pat dough into a 12x9-inch rectangle. Starting with one short side, roll up dough into a log, pressing seam to seal. Place log, seam side down, in prepared pan. Cover and let rise in a warm, draft-free place (75°F/24°C) until doubled in size, 1 to 1½ hours.
6. Preheat oven to 350°F (180°C).
7. Brush egg white onto dough.
8. Bake until top is golden brown and an instant-read thermometer inserted in center registers 200°F (93°C), 45 to 50 minutes, loosely covering with foil after 25 minutes of baking to prevent excess browning. Let cool in pan for 10 minutes. Using excess parchment as handles, remove from pan, and let cool completely on a wire rack. Store in an airtight container for up to 3 days.

Cranberry-Walnut Bread

Make 1 (13-inch) loaf

This bread recipe calls for adding a pan of water to the oven while baking. The resulting steam keeps the surface of your dough moist and flexible, delaying crust formation during the early stages of baking so your bread can rise beautifully. This creates a more open interior and a crisper crust.

4¾ cups (603 grams) bread flour
4 teaspoons (12 grams) kosher salt
2¼ teaspoons (7 grams) instant yeast
1 cup (128 grams) unsweetened dried cranberries
1 cup (113 grams) chopped toasted walnuts
2 cups (480 grams) warm water (105°F/41°C to 110°F/43°C)
2 tablespoons (42 grams) honey
Semolina flour, for dusting
4 cups (960 grams) boiling water

1. In the bowl of a stand mixer, whisk together bread flour, salt, and yeast by hand; stir in cranberries and walnuts. Add 2 cups (480 grams) warm water and honey; using the paddle attachment, beat at low speed until a sticky dough forms, about 30 seconds.
2. Spray a large bowl with cooking spray. Place dough in bowl, turning to grease top. Cover and let stand in a warm, draft-free place (75°F/24°C) until doubled in size, 1½ to 2 hours. Refrigerate for at least 2 hours or up to overnight.
3. Line a large baking sheet with parchment paper; dust parchment with semolina flour.
4. Heavily dust a work surface with bread flour; turn out dough onto prepared surface. Using floured hands, lightly press dough into a 15x10-inch rectangle. Starting with one short side, roll up dough into a log, pressing edges to seal. Place log, seam side down, on prepared pan. Sprinkle semolina flour on top of dough. Loosely cover dough with a greased sheet of plastic wrap, and let rise in a warm, draft-free place (75°F/24°C) until puffed, 1 to 1½ hours.
5. Position oven racks in bottom and center of oven. Preheat oven to 500°F (260°C).
6. Score top of dough as desired. Place on center oven rack. Carefully place 4 cups (960 grams) boiling water in a baking pan on bottom oven rack. Immediately reduce oven temperature to 425°F (220°C).
7. Bake for 20 minutes. Loosely cover with foil, and bake until an instant-read thermometer inserted in center registers 200°F (93°C), 20 to 25 minutes more. Remove from pan, and let cool completely on a wire rack. Store in an airtight container for up to 3 days.

Hot Cross Buns

Makes 12 buns

My take on the British classic has all the hallmarks of the original, bursting with sweet currants, candied orange peel, and warm spices and adorned with a striking cross. Still, I made a few tasty twists, incorporating rich butter and aromatic orange blossom water into the flour paste cross. It's the perfect bite of time-honored taste and tradition.

- **1 cup (128 grams) dried currants**
- **¾ cup (180 grams) very hot fresh orange juice (180°F/82°C to 185°F/85°C)**
- **¾ cup (180 grams) warm whole milk (105°F/41°C to 110°F/43°C)**
- **½ cup (120 grams) warm water (105°F/41°C to 110°F/43°C)**
- **½ cup (100 grams) granulated sugar, divided**
- **1½ tablespoons (14 grams) active dry yeast**
- **5⅔ cups (708 grams) plus ½ cup (63 grams) all-purpose flour, divided**
- **1 teaspoon kosher salt**
- **1 teaspoon ground cinnamon**
- **½ teaspoon ground nutmeg**
- **¼ teaspoon ground allspice**
- **⅓ cup (76 grams) unsalted butter, melted**
- **3 large eggs (150 grams), room temperature and divided**
- **⅔ cup (90 grams) chopped candied orange peel**
- **5 tablespoons (70 grams) unsalted butter, room temperature**
- **1 teaspoon orange blossom water**
- **½ teaspoon water**

1. In a medium bowl, combine currants and very hot orange juice. Cover with plastic wrap, and let stand for 20 minutes. Using a fine-mesh sieve, strain currants, discarding excess liquid.

2. In the bowl of a stand mixer, whisk together warm milk, ½ cup (120 grams) warm water, ¼ cup (50 grams) sugar, and yeast by hand. Let stand until foamy, about 10 minutes.

3. In a large bowl, whisk together 2⅔ cups (333 grams) flour, salt, cinnamon, nutmeg, allspice, and remaining ¼ cup (50 grams) sugar. Add flour mixture to yeast mixture; using the paddle attachment, beat at low speed just until combined. Beat in melted butter and 2 eggs (100 grams). Add currants and candied orange peel, and beat until combined. Gradually add 2⅔ cups (333 grams) flour, beating until combined; scrape sides of bowl.

4. Switch to the dough hook attachment. Beat at low speed until a smooth, elastic, slightly tacky dough forms, 4 to 6 minutes; add up to ⅓ cup (42 grams) flour, 1 tablespoon (8 grams) at a time, if dough is too sticky. Turn out dough onto a lightly floured surface, and shape into a smooth round.

5. Spray a large bowl with cooking spray. Place dough in bowl, turning to grease top. Loosely cover and let rise in a warm, draft-free place (75°F/24°C) until doubled in size, about 1 hour.

6. Spray a 13x9-inch rimmed baking sheet with baking spray with flour.

7. Lightly punch down dough, and let stand for 5 minutes. Turn out dough onto a lightly floured surface, and divide into 12 portions (about 128 grams each). Roll each portion into a ball. Place about ¼ inch apart on prepared pan. Cover and let rise in a warm, draft-free place (75°F/24°C) until puffed, buns are touching, and dough holds an indentation when pressed, about 40 minutes.

8. Preheat oven to 375°F (190°C).

9. In a small bowl, whisk remaining 1 egg (50 grams). Brush egg on top of rolls.

10. Clean bowl of stand mixer and paddle attachment. Using the paddle attachment, beat room temperature butter and remaining ½ cup (63 grams) flour at medium-low speed; slowly add orange blossom water and ½ teaspoon water, beating until a thick paste forms and stopping to scrape sides of bowl. Spoon paste into a pastry bag, and cut a ¼-inch opening in tip. (Alternatively, use a pastry bag fitted with a ¼-inch round piping tip [Ateco #802].) Pipe paste on top of buns in continuous lines, following curves of rolls, to form a cross over each.

11. Bake until golden brown and an instant-read thermometer inserted in center registers 190°F (88°C) to 200°F (93°C), 24 to 30 minutes, loosely covering with foil during final 2 to 5 minutes of baking to prevent excess browning. Serve warm or at room temperature.

Panettone

Makes 1 (15-ounce) loaf

Panettone begins with a *biga*, a firm preferment of flour, water, and yeast. As it rests, flour hydrates and gluten begins organizing before butter, egg yolks, and sugar—ingredients that can weaken gluten—are added. This early structure helps the enriched dough rise tall and form panettone's signature shreddable crumb.

Soaked fruits:
¼ cup (40 grams) golden raisins
¼ cup (40 grams) chopped dried cherries
¼ cup (60 grams) dark spiced rum
2 tablespoons (20 grams) diced candied orange peel

Biga:
2 tablespoons (30 grams) lukewarm water (85°F/29°C to 90°F/32°C)
2¼ teaspoons (7 grams) active dry yeast
6 tablespoons (48 grams) bread flour

Dough:
1¼ cups (159 grams) bread flour
¼ cup (50 grams) granulated sugar
1½ teaspoons (5 grams) kosher salt
¼ cup (60 grams) whole milk, room temperature
2 large egg yolks (37 grams), room temperature
1 teaspoon orange zest
1 teaspoon vanilla extract
5 tablespoons (70 grams) unsalted butter, cubed and room temperature
⅔ cup (113 grams) 55% to 65% cacao semisweet chocolate chips (optional)

1 large egg (50 grams)
1 tablespoon (15 grams) water
2 teaspoons (8 grams) Swedish pearl sugar
1 tablespoon (14 grams) unsalted butter, cut into very small pieces, room temperature

1. For soaked fruits: In a medium bowl, toss together all ingredients. Cover and let stand overnight.
2. For biga: In the bowl of a stand mixer, whisk together 2 tablespoons (30 grams) lukewarm water and yeast by hand until yeast dissolves. Add flour; stir with a rubber spatula until combined and a shaggy dough forms. Knead dough in bowl by hand until combined. Cover and let rise in a warm, draft-free place (75°F/24°C) until doubled in size, 20 to 30 minutes.
3. For dough: Add flour, granulated sugar, and salt to biga. Add milk, egg yolks, orange zest, and vanilla. Using the dough hook attachment, beat at medium-low speed until a slightly tacky, smooth, and elastic dough forms, 12 to 15 minutes, stopping to scrape sides of bowl. (Dough should pass the windowpane test; see page 16.)
4. With mixer on low speed, add cubed butter, 1 tablespoon (14 grams) at a time, beating until combined after each addition (about 5 minutes total). Beat until all butter is fully incorporated and dough passes windowpane test, 10 to 15 minutes. (See page 16.)
5. Turn out dough onto a clean surface, and shape into a smooth round. Place in a clean bowl. Cover and let rise in a warm, draft-free place (75°F/24°C) until doubled in size, 1½ to 2 hours.
6. Drain soaked fruits, and pat dry with paper towels.
7. Turn out dough onto a clean surface, and flatten into a ½-inch-thick round. Sprinkle half of soaked fruits or half of chocolate chips (if using) onto dough. Using a rolling pin, press fruit or chocolate into dough.
8. Fold dough in half. Rotate dough 90 degrees. Roll dough into a ½-inch-thick round. Sprinkle remaining soaked fruits or chocolate chips onto dough. Press fruit or chocolate into dough; fold dough in half. Gently knead dough until all fruit or chocolate is well distributed. Shape into a round, and return to ungreased bowl. Cover and refrigerate for at least 8 hours or up to overnight.
9. Let covered dough stand at room temperature for 1½ to 2 hours.
10. Insert 2 (12-inch) bamboo skewers parallel through bottom of a 15-ounce paper panettone mold. (There should be an even amount of skewer showing on each side of the mold.)
11. Turn out dough onto a clean surface, and flatten into a ½-inch-thick round. Lift bottom side of dough, and gently stretch and fold bottom third over center third. Stretch right side out, and fold over center third; repeat with left side. Fold top third over previous folds. Roll dough away from you, and using both hands, cup dough and pull it toward you to seal. Rotate dough 90 degrees, and pull again, repeating until a tight, smooth boule forms. Place, seam side down, into

prepared mold, and place mold on a rimmed baking sheet. Cover and let rise in a warm, draft-free place (75°F/24°C) until doubled in size, 1½ to 2 hours.

12. Preheat oven to 350°F (180°C).

13. In a small bowl, whisk together egg and 1 tablespoon (15 grams) water; brush onto dough. Sprinkle with pearl sugar. Using a lame or sharp paring knife, score top of dough with an "X." Place small butter pieces in scored "X."

14. Bake until golden brown and an instant-read thermometer inserted in center registers 190°F (88°C), about 40 minutes, covering with foil halfway through baking to prevent excess browning. Immediately invert loaf, and place over a tall bowl (such as the bowl of a stand mixer), placing skewers on edge of bowl; let cool completely upside down. Store in an airtight container for up to 2 weeks.

Baklava Monkey Bread

Makes 1 (9-inch) loaf

I coated soft, bite-size rounds of dough in a mixture of honey, nuts, and fragrant spices to create a decadent twist on the classic Mediterranean and Middle Eastern pastry.

Dough:
- ¾ cup (180 grams) warm whole milk (100°F/38°C to 110°F/43°C)
- 1½ tablespoons (18 grams) granulated sugar, divided
- 1 tablespoon (9 grams) active dry yeast
- 3¼ cups (413 grams) bread flour
- 2¼ teaspoons (7 grams) kosher salt
- ⅓ cup (76 grams) unsalted butter, melted
- 1 large egg (50 grams), room temperature
- 1 large egg yolk (19 grams), room temperature
- 1½ tablespoons (32 grams) honey

Syrup:
- ½ cup (110 grams) firmly packed light brown sugar
- ⅓ cup (80 grams) heavy whipping cream
- ¼ cup (85 grams) honey
- 2 tablespoons (28 grams) unsalted butter
- ½ teaspoon lemon zest
- ½ teaspoon orange blossom water
- ¼ teaspoon kosher salt

Topping:
- ½ cup (100 grams) granulated sugar
- 1 teaspoon ground cinnamon
- ¼ teaspoon ground cloves
- ½ cup (70 grams) pistachios, finely chopped
- ½ cup (55 grams) walnuts, finely chopped

1. For dough: In a small bowl, stir together warm milk, ½ tablespoon (6 grams) sugar, and yeast. Let stand until foamy, 5 to 10 minutes.
2. In the bowl of a stand mixer, whisk together flour, salt, and remaining 1 tablespoon (12 grams) sugar by hand until combined. Add yeast mixture, melted butter, egg, egg yolk, and honey; using the paddle attachment, beat at low speed until a shaggy dough forms, 1 to 2 minutes.
3. Switch to the dough hook attachment. Beat at medium-low speed until a smooth, elastic dough forms, 6 to 8 minutes.
4. Spray a large bowl with cooking spray. Place dough in bowl, turning to grease top. Cover and let rise in a warm, draft-free place (75°F/24°C) until doubled in size, 35 to 45 minutes.
5. For syrup: In a medium saucepan, bring brown sugar, cream, honey, butter, lemon zest, orange blossom water, and salt to a boil over medium-high heat, stirring frequently until sugar dissolves. Remove from heat; keep warm but not hot.
6. For topping: In a medium bowl, whisk together granulated sugar, cinnamon, and cloves. In another small bowl, stir together pistachios and walnuts.
7. Punch down dough; let stand for 5 minutes.
8. Spray a tall-sided 9-inch round cake pan with baking spray with flour. (See Note.)
9. On a clean surface, divide dough into 40 portions (about 20 grams each); gently shape each portion into a ball, pinching closed any seams if needed. (Keep dough portions covered with plastic wrap while working.)
10. Spoon one-third of warm syrup (about ⅓ cup or 95 grams) into bottom of prepared pan. Sprinkle ½ cup (65 grams) nut mixture onto syrup in pan.
11. Working in batches, toss dough portions in granulated sugar mixture. (There will be granulated sugar mixture left over.) Place half of dough (about 20 portions) in pan. Top with half of syrup and remaining nut mixture. Layer remaining dough portions on top and between open spaces; drizzle with remaining syrup. Cover and let rise in a warm, draft-free place (75°F/24°C) until puffed, about 30 minutes.
12. Preheat oven to 350°F (180°C).
13. Bake until golden brown and an instant-read thermometer inserted in center registers at least 190°F (88°C), about 45 minutes, covering with foil after 30 minutes of baking to prevent excess browning. Let cool in pan for 5 minutes. Invert onto a serving plate. Best served warm. Store in an airtight container for up to 2 days.

Note: *At least a 3-inch-tall pan is needed to protect the edges from overbaking and to keep syrup from spilling over. A 2-inch-tall pan can be used, but you'll need to place the pan on a parchment paper-lined baking sheet to catch any overflow and cover bread with foil halfway through baking to prevent excess browning.*

Greek Feta Bread

Makes 1 (13-inch) loaf

Called *tiropsomo* in Greek, which translates to "cheese bread," this hand-shaped and stuffed flatbread is commonly eaten as a grab-and-go breakfast or an afternoon snack.

4¾ cups (594 grams) all-purpose flour
1½ cups (360 grams) hot water (120°F/49°C to 130°F/54°C)
¼ cup (56 grams) plus 2 tablespoons (28 grams) olive oil, divided
1 tablespoon (12 grams) granulated sugar
1 tablespoon (9 grams) kosher salt
2¼ teaspoons (7 grams) instant yeast
14 ounces (400 grams) creamy feta cheese (see Note)
1½ tablespoons (2 grams) chopped fresh parsley
1 tablespoon (1 gram) chopped fresh dill
Sesame seeds, for sprinkling

1. In the bowl of a stand mixer fitted with the paddle attachment, beat flour, 1½ cups (360 grams) hot water, ¼ cup (56 grams) oil, sugar, salt, and yeast at low speed until a shaggy dough forms, about 2 minutes.
2. Switch to the dough hook attachment. Beat at medium-low speed until a smooth, elastic dough forms, about 10 minutes. (Dough will be very soft but should not be overly sticky.)
3. Oil a large bowl. Place dough in bowl, turning to grease top. Cover with plastic wrap, and let rise in a warm, draft-free place (75°F/24°C) until doubled in size, about 30 minutes.
4. Line a rimmed baking sheet with parchment paper.
5. Turn out dough onto a lightly floured surface, and pat into a 15-inch circle that is thinner around edges than in center. Crumble feta onto dough, leaving a 1-inch border around edges; sprinkle parsley and dill onto feta. Lightly press into dough to adhere. Fold sides of dough over filling to center, pinching seams to seal. Carefully turn dough over, and place on prepared pan. Press dough into a 13x10-inch rectangle. Cover and let rise in a warm, draft-free place (75°F/24°C) until puffed, about 45 minutes.
6. Preheat oven to 425°F (220°C).
7. Brush remaining 2 tablespoons (28 grams) oil onto dough; sprinkle sesame seeds on top. Using your fingertips, dimple dough and flatten any air pockets.
8. Bake until golden brown and an instant-read thermometer inserted in center registers 190°F (88°C), 15 to 20 minutes. Let cool on pan on a wire rack for 10 to 15 minutes. Serve warm or at room temperature.

Note: *Creamy feta cheese is softer in texture and crumbles more easily than standard feta, though it is not the same as pre-crumbled feta. Creamy feta can sometimes be labeled as French feta.*

Spinach-Artichoke Pretzel Buns

Makes 12 buns

Pillowy-soft pretzel buns are filled with a generous helping of cheesy spinach-artichoke mixture, sprinkled with sesame seeds, and baked to golden perfection, irresistibly combining dip and dipper.

Dough:
4¼ cups (531 grams) all-purpose flour, divided
1 tablespoon (12 grams) granulated sugar
1 tablespoon (9 grams) kosher salt
2¼ teaspoons (7 grams) instant yeast
1 cup (240 grams) water
½ cup (120 grams) whole milk
2 tablespoons (28 grams) unsalted butter

Filling:
4 ounces (113 grams) cream cheese, softened
½ teaspoon garlic powder
½ teaspoon ground black pepper
¼ teaspoon kosher salt
¼ teaspoon crushed red pepper, optional
2 ounces (57 grams) mozzarella cheese, shredded
2 ounces (57 grams) Parmesan cheese, shredded
½ cup (85 grams) drained thawed frozen chopped spinach
½ cup (80 grams) drained quartered artichoke hearts, chopped

8 cups (1,920 grams) water
⅓ cup (80 grams) baking soda
Coarse salt and sesame seeds, for sprinkling

1. For dough: In the bowl of a stand mixer, whisk together 2 cups (250 grams) flour, sugar, kosher salt, and yeast by hand until combined.
2. In a small saucepan, heat 1 cup (240 grams) water, milk, and butter over medium heat until an instant-read thermometer registers 120°F (49°C) to 130°F (54°C). Add hot milk mixture to flour mixture; using the paddle attachment, beat at medium-low speed until combined, about 1 minute. With mixer on low speed, gradually add remaining 2¼ cups (281 grams) flour, beating just until combined and stopping to scrape sides of bowl.
3. Switch to the dough hook attachment. Beat at low speed until a soft, somewhat tacky dough forms, 10 to 12 minutes, stopping to scrape dough hook and sides of bowl. (Dough will mostly pull away from sides of bowl and should pass the windowpane test; see page 16.) Shape dough into a smooth round.
4. Lightly oil a large bowl. Place dough in bowl, turning to grease top. Cover and let rise in a warm, draft-free place (75°F/24°C) until doubled in size, 45 minutes to 1 hour.
5. For filling: In a medium bowl, stir together cream cheese, garlic powder, black pepper, salt, and red pepper until smooth; stir in mozzarella and Parmesan. Fold in spinach and artichokes. Cover and refrigerate until ready to use.
6. Cut 12 (6x5¼-inch) rectangles of parchment paper. Place rectangles on rimmed baking sheets; dust with flour.
7. On a clean surface, divide dough into 12 portions (about 75 grams each). Gently deflate 1 portion of dough to release any large air bubbles, and shape into a round. (Keep remaining dough covered to prevent it from drying out.) Place on a prepared parchment rectangle. Repeat with remaining dough. Cover and let rise in a warm, draft-free place (75°F/24°C) until puffed, 30 to 45 minutes.
8. Preheat oven to 375°F (190°C).
9. In a medium saucepan, bring 8 cups (1,920 grams) water and baking soda to a low boil over medium-low heat.
10. Using parchment to transfer, carefully lower dough rounds, 1 or 2 at a time, top side down, into boiling water-baking soda mixture; discard parchment. Cook for 30 seconds per side. Remove dough using a large slotted spatula or spoon, letting excess water drip off; place 1 inch apart on nonstick baking sheets.
11. Gently press down center of each dough round. Spoon about 1½ tablespoons (32 grams) filling into each indentation. Sprinkle with coarse salt and sesame seeds.
12. Bake, one pan at a time, until golden brown, 12 to 16 minutes. Let cool on pans for 5 minutes. Serve warm or at room temperature. Refrigerate in an airtight container for up to 3 days.

Pan de Jamón

Makes 1 (15-inch) loaf

This loaf encases thinly sliced ham, briny olives, and chewy raisins. Somewhere between sweet and savory, this bread is great as a meal in its own right.

---

4 cups (500 grams) all-purpose flour, divided
¼ cup (50 grams) granulated sugar
2¼ teaspoons (7 grams) instant yeast
1½ teaspoons (5 grams) kosher salt
½ cup (120 grams) water
½ cup (120 grams) whole milk
¼ cup (57 grams) unsalted butter
3 large eggs (150 grams), divided
1 (5.75-ounce) jar (163 grams) pimiento-stuffed green olives
8 ounces (226 grams) deli-sliced ham (about 9 slices)
¼ cup (32 grams) raisins

1. In the bowl of a stand mixer fitted with the paddle attachment, beat 2 cups (250 grams) flour, sugar, yeast, and salt at low speed until combined.
2. In a medium saucepan, heat ½ cup (120 grams) water, milk, and butter over medium-low heat until butter is melted and an instant-read thermometer registers 120°F (49°C) to 130°F (54°C). Add hot milk mixture to flour mixture, and beat at low speed until combined, about 1 minute. Add 2 eggs (100 grams), and beat for 1 minute. Add remaining 2 cups (250 grams) flour, and beat until a shaggy dough forms.
3. Switch to the dough hook attachment. Beat at low speed until dough is soft, smooth, and elastic, 8 to 10 minutes. Turn out dough onto a clean surface, and shape into a ball.
4. Spray a medium bowl with cooking spray. Place dough in bowl, turning to grease top. Cover and let rise in a warm, draft-free place (75°F/24°C) until doubled in size, about 45 minutes.
5. Drain olives, and place on a paper towel-lined baking sheet; pat dry. Place ham on another paper towel-lined baking sheet; pat dry.
6. Line a rimmed baking sheet with parchment paper.
7. Punch down dough; loosely cover and let stand for 10 minutes. On a lightly floured surface, roll dough into a 15x10-inch rectangle (about ½ inch thick). Arrange ham on top of dough, leaving a ¼-inch border on all sides. Sprinkle olives and raisins onto ham. Starting with one long side, roll up dough into a log; pinch seam to seal. Place, seam side down, on prepared pan. Pinch ends closed, and tuck under. Cover and let rise in a warm, draft-free place (75°F/24°C) until doubled in size, 30 to 40 minutes.
8. Preheat oven to 375°F (190°C).
9. In a small bowl, lightly whisk remaining 1 egg (50 grams). Brush egg wash on top and sides of dough.
10. Bake until golden brown, 20 to 25 minutes. Let cool on pan for 25 minutes; serve warm or at room temperature.

Caprese Pull-Apart Loaf

Makes 1 (9x5-inch) loaf

The word "caprese" instantly denotes fresh tomato, basil, and mozzarella served as an appetizer or salad. This iteration makes use of oil-packed sun-dried tomatoes, chopped basil, and shredded fresh mozzarella layered between thin pieces of dough that bake up golden brown on the outside, burst with flavor on the inside, and should absolutely be shared.

2½ cups (313 grams) all-purpose flour, divided
2 tablespoons (24 grams) granulated sugar
2¼ teaspoons (7 grams) instant yeast
2 teaspoons (6 grams) kosher salt
¾ cup (180 grams) whole milk
3 tablespoons (42 grams) olive oil
1 large egg (50 grams), room temperature
2 tablespoons (28 grams) unsalted butter, melted
2 cloves garlic (3 grams), minced
1 (8-ounce) ball (226 grams) fresh mozzarella cheese, shredded
½ cup (80 grams) drained oil-packed sun-dried tomatoes, chopped
¼ cup (10 grams) chopped fresh basil
Garnish: fresh basil, sun-dried tomato oil

1. In the bowl of a stand mixer, whisk together 1 cup (125 grams) flour, sugar, yeast, and salt by hand.
2. In a medium saucepan, heat milk over medium heat until an instant-read thermometer registers 120°F (49°C) to 130°F (54°C).
3. Using the paddle attachment, with mixer on medium speed, add hot milk and olive oil to flour mixture, beating until combined, about 1 minute. Add egg, and beat until combined. With mixer on low speed, gradually add remaining 1½ cups (188 grams) flour, beating until well combined and stopping to scrape sides of bowl, about 1 minute.
4. Switch to the dough hook attachment. Beat at medium speed until dough is smooth and elastic and pulls away from sides of bowl, 10 to 15 minutes.
5. Lightly spray a large bowl. Place dough in bowl, turning to grease top. Cover and let rise in a warm, draft-free place (75°F/24°C) until doubled in size, 45 minutes to 1 hour.
6. In a small bowl, stir together melted butter and garlic.
7. Spray a 9x5-inch loaf pan with baking spray with flour. Line pan with parchment paper, letting excess extend over long sides of pan.
8. On a lightly floured surface, roll dough into a 16x12-inch rectangle (about ¼ inch thick), with one long side closest to you. Using a pastry brush, brush butter mixture onto dough. Top with mozzarella, tomatoes, and basil. Cut dough into 16 rectangles (about 4x3 inches each).
9. Stand prepared pan vertically on one short side. Starting at bottom, carefully layer dough pieces, filling side up, one on top of the other. For final piece of dough, place in pan filling side down. Turn pan upright onto its bottom. Cover and let rise in a warm, draft-free place (75°F/24°C) until doubled in size, 20 to 25 minutes.
10. Preheat oven to 350°F (180°C).
11. Tuck any exposed tomatoes inside dough pieces.
12. Bake until golden brown and an instant-read thermometer inserted in center registers 190°F (88°C), 45 to 50 minutes. Let cool in pan for 10 minutes. Using excess parchment as handles, remove from pan, and let cool on a wire rack for 10 minutes. Garnish with torn basil and tomato oil, if desired. Serve warm.

BRAIDED and TWISTED

Explore how indulgent ingredients come together with fun shaping techniques to create Eastern European babka, Swedish buns, Mexican *pan de muerto*, and more

Everything Pretzels

Makes 12 pretzels

Once you make these chewy pretzels, you'll never want to buy them again.

½ cup (120 grams) warm water (110°F/43°C to 115°F/46°C)
3 teaspoons (8 grams) granulated sugar, divided
2¼ teaspoons (7 grams) instant yeast
4¼ cups (531 grams) all-purpose flour, divided
1 tablespoon (9 grams) kosher salt
1 cup (240 grams) warm whole milk (110°F/43°C to 115°F/46°C)
2 tablespoons (28 grams) unsalted butter, melted
8 cups (1,920 grams) water
¼ cup (60 grams) baking soda
Everything bagel seasoning, for sprinkling

1. In a small bowl, whisk together ½ cup (120 grams) warm water, 1 teaspoon sugar, and yeast. Let stand until foamy, 5 to 10 minutes.
2. In the bowl of a stand mixer fitted with the paddle attachment, beat 2 cups (250 grams) flour, salt, and remaining 2 teaspoons (8 grams) sugar at low speed until combined. Add yeast mixture, warm milk, and melted butter; beat at medium-low speed until combined, about 1 minute, stopping to scrape sides of bowl. With mixer on low speed, gradually add remaining 2¼ cups (281 grams) flour, beating just until combined and stopping to scrape sides of bowl.
3. Switch to the dough hook attachment. Beat at low speed until a soft, somewhat tacky dough forms, 10 to 12 minutes, stopping to scrape dough hook and sides of bowl. (Dough will mostly pull away from sides of bowl and should pass the windowpane test; see page 16). Shape dough into a smooth round.
4. Lightly oil a large bowl. Place dough in bowl, turning to grease top. Cover and let rise in a warm, draft-free place (75°F/24°C) until doubled in size, 45 minutes to 1 hour.
5. Cut 12 (6x5¼-inch) rectangles of parchment paper; place rectangles on 2 rimmed baking sheets, and dust with flour.
6. On a clean surface, divide dough into 12 portions (about 76 grams each). Gently deflate 1 portion to release any large air bubbles. (Keep remaining dough covered to prevent it from drying out.) Roll into a 24-inch-long strand that tapers at each end. Shape into a "U"; cross strand 3 inches from ends. Twist ends around each other once, and fold down so loose ends touch rounded part of "U" shape just to sides of center; gently press to secure, and carefully stretch to open pretzel shape, if necessary. Place on a prepared parchment rectangle. Repeat with remaining dough. Cover and let rise in a warm, draft-free place (75°F/24°C) until puffed, 30 to 45 minutes.
7. Preheat oven to 375°F (190°C). Line 2 baking sheets with parchment paper.
8. In a medium saucepan, bring 8 cups (1,920 grams) water and baking soda to a low boil over medium-low heat.
9. Using parchment rectangles to transfer, carefully lower pretzels, 1 or 2 at a time, top side down, into boiling water-baking soda mixture; discard parchment. Cook for 10 seconds per side. Remove dough using a large slotted spatula or spoon, letting excess water drip off; place 1 inch apart on prepared pans. Sprinkle with everything bagel seasoning.
10. Bake, one pan at a time, until deep golden brown, 12 to 16 minutes. Let cool on pan for 5 minutes. Serve warm or at room temperature. Store in an airtight container for up to 3 days.

Sesame-and-Green Onion Knots

Makes 12 rolls

Studded with green onion (a.k.a. scallions or spring onions) and sesame seeds, these rolls are inspired by *cong you bing* (scallion pancakes), a savory Chinese flatbread.

---

4 to 4¼ cups (508 to 540 grams) bread flour, divided
2 tablespoons (24 grams) granulated sugar
1 tablespoon (9 grams) plus ¼ teaspoon kosher salt, divided
2¼ teaspoons (7 grams) instant yeast
¾ cup (180 grams) whole milk
½ cup (120 grams) plus 1 tablespoon (15 grams) water, divided
⅓ cup (76 grams) unsalted butter
2 large eggs (100 grams), room temperature and divided
¾ cup (64 grams) lightly packed finely sliced green onion
1½ teaspoons (7 grams) sesame oil
1 teaspoon minced garlic
3 tablespoons (42 grams) unsalted butter, melted and cooled slightly
Sesame seeds, for sprinkling

1. In the bowl of a stand mixer, whisk together 2 cups (254 grams) flour, sugar, 1 tablespoon (9 grams) salt, and yeast by hand.
2. In a medium saucepan, heat milk, ½ cup (120 grams) water, and butter over medium heat until an instant-read thermometer registers 120°F (49°C) to 130°F (54°C). Add hot milk mixture to flour mixture; using the paddle attachment, beat at medium speed until combined. Add 1 egg (50 grams), beating until combined. With mixer on low speed, gradually add 2 cups (254 grams) flour, beating just until a shaggy dough comes together and stopping to scrape sides of bowl.
3. Switch to the dough hook attachment. Beat at low speed until a soft, smooth, somewhat sticky dough forms, 20 to 23 minutes; add up to remaining ¼ cup (32 grams) flour, 1 tablespoon (8 grams) at a time, if dough is too sticky. Turn out dough onto a lightly floured surface, and shape into a smooth round.
4. Lightly oil a large bowl. Place dough in bowl, turning to grease top. Cover and let rise in a warm, draft-free place (75°F/24°C) until doubled in size, 40 minutes to 1 hour.
5. Spray a 12-cup muffin pan with baking spray with flour.
6. Punch down dough, and let stand for 5 minutes. On a lightly floured surface, roll dough into an 18x12-inch rectangle, with one long side closest to you.
7. In a small bowl, stir together green onion, sesame oil, garlic, and remaining ¼ teaspoon salt.
8. Using a pastry brush, brush melted butter onto dough. Sprinkle green onion mixture evenly onto bottom half of dough, leaving a ½-inch border along bottom long side. Fold top half down, lightly pressing to adhere. Trim ⅛ to ¼ inch off short sides of dough; cut crosswise into 12 strips (about 1½ inches wide each).
9. Leaving ½ inch intact at folded end, cut 1 dough strip into 3 strands. Loosely braid strands, pinching end to adhere. Carefully tuck loose end of braid under to create a knot. Place in a prepared muffin cup. Repeat with remaining dough strips. Cover and let rise in a warm, draft-free place (75°F/24°C) until puffed, 30 to 45 minutes.
10. Preheat oven to 375°F (190°C).
11. In another small bowl, whisk together remaining 1 egg (50 grams) and remaining 1 tablespoon (15 grams) water. Using a pastry brush, gently brush egg wash onto rolls; sprinkle with sesame seeds.
12. Bake until golden brown and an instant-read thermometer inserted in center registers at least 190°F (88°C), about 20 minutes. Let cool in pan on a wire rack for 10 minutes. Serve warm. Store in an airtight container for up to 3 days.

Tarte Soleil

Makes 1 (14-inch) loaf

Named after its shape, *tarte soleil* (which translates to "sun bread") is as delicious as it is beautiful. Traditionally enjoyed during *apéro,* the French term for cocktail hour, the bread's twisted strands allow it to be easily pulled apart, making it perfect to share with friends.

Garlic-herb butter:

- 1 medium head garlic (65 grams)
- 1 teaspoon olive oil
- 1 teaspoon kosher salt, divided
- ½ cup (10 grams) lightly packed fresh parsley leaves
- ¼ cup (6 grams) lightly packed sliced fresh chives
- 2 tablespoons (3 grams) fresh rosemary leaves
- ⅔ cup (150 grams) unsalted butter, room temperature
- ¼ teaspoon finely ground black pepper

Dough:

- 3¼ cups plus 2 tablespoons (422 grams) all-purpose flour, divided
- 1 tablespoon (12 grams) granulated sugar
- 2¼ teaspoons (7 grams) instant yeast
- 2 teaspoons (6 grams) kosher salt
- 1 cup (240 grams) whole milk
- ¼ cup (57 grams) unsalted butter, softened
- 1 large egg (50 grams), room temperature

- 1 large egg (50 grams)
- 1 tablespoon (15 grams) water
- 2 teaspoons (6 grams) sesame seeds
- 1 tablespoon (14 grams) unsalted butter, melted and warm

1. Preheat oven to 400°F (200°C).
2. For garlic-herb butter: Cut ¼ inch off top end of garlic, keeping cloves intact. Place garlic, cut side up, on a piece of foil. Drizzle with oil, and sprinkle with ⅛ teaspoon salt. Wrap in foil.
3. Bake until fragrant and deep golden brown, about 45 minutes. Unwrap garlic, and let cool completely.
4. Squeeze garlic pulp into the work bowl of a food processor; add parsley, chives, and rosemary, and process until almost smooth, 1 to 2 minutes, stopping to scrape sides of bowl. Add room temperature butter, pepper, and remaining ¾ teaspoon plus ⅛ teaspoon salt, and process until smooth and creamy, 1 to 2 minutes, stopping to scrape sides of bowl. Refrigerate in airtight container for up to 3 days. Let come to room temperature before using.
5. For dough: In the bowl of a stand mixer fitted with the paddle attachment, beat 1 cup (125 grams) flour, sugar, yeast, and salt at medium-low speed until well combined, stopping to scrape sides of bowl.
6. In a medium saucepan, heat milk and softened butter over medium heat until an instant-read thermometer registers 120°F (49°C) to 130°F (54°C). Add hot milk mixture to flour mixture; beat at medium speed for 2 minutes, stopping to scrape sides of bowl. Add room temperature egg; beat at medium-high speed for 2 minutes. With mixer on low speed, gradually add remaining 2¼ cups plus 2 tablespoons (297 grams) flour, beating just until combined and stopping to scrape sides of bowl.
7. Switch to the dough hook attachment. Beat at medium speed until a soft, somewhat sticky dough forms, about 15 minutes, stopping to scrape dough hook and sides of bowl. (Dough may still stick slightly to sides of bowl but should pass the windowpane test; see page 16.)
8. Spray a large bowl with cooking spray. Place dough in bowl, turning to grease top. Cover and let rise in a warm, draft-free place (75°F/24°C) until doubled in size, 40 minutes to 1 hour.
9. Line a large light-colored rimmed baking sheet with parchment paper.
10. Lightly punch down dough; cover and let stand for 5 minutes. Turn out dough, and divide into 4 portions (about 190 grams each); gently shape each into a ball. Cover with plastic wrap, and let stand for 15 minutes.
11. Keeping other portions covered with plastic wrap, roll and pat 1 dough ball into an 11-inch circle; gently place on prepared pan. (Dough may shrink slightly.) Spread one-third of garlic-herb butter (about ¼ cup or 55 grams) onto dough circle, leaving a ½-inch border around edges. Repeat with 2 dough balls and remaining butter, stacking layers. Roll remaining dough ball into an 11-inch circle, and place on top of previous layers.
12. Place a 1½-inch round cutter in center of dough; gently press down just to leave a mark. Using a sharp knife or a pizza cutter, make 16 evenly spaced cuts from center mark to edge of dough. Grasping 1 cut piece at a time, twist portion to the right 3 to 4 times; pinch ends

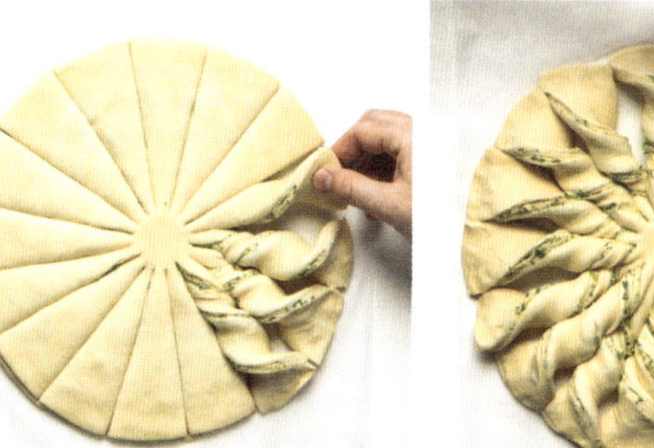

firmly together to adhere. Repeat with remaining cut portions. Cover and let rise in a warm, draft-free place (75°F/24°C) until nearly doubled in size, 30 to 45 minutes.

13. Preheat oven to 375°F (190°C).

14. In a small bowl, whisk together egg and 1 tablespoon (15 grams) water; brush onto dough, and sprinkle sesame seeds in center. Pinch ends together again, if necessary.

15. Bake until golden brown and an instant-read thermometer inserted in center registers at least 190°F (88°C), 18 to 22 minutes, lightly covering with foil to prevent excess browning, if necessary. Let cool on pan for 15 minutes. Brush with melted butter. Best served warm. Store in an airtight container for up to 2 days.

Chocolate Babka

Makes 1 (8½x4½-inch) loaf

This chocolate-filled affair is the quintessential babka, brushed with syrup for sweet shine. When your nostalgic heart calls for babka, this is the recipe to turn to.

Dough:

- 2½ cups (313 grams) plus 2 tablespoons (16 grams) all-purpose flour, divided
- 3 tablespoons (36 grams) granulated sugar
- 1½ teaspoons (5 grams) instant yeast
- 1¼ teaspoons (4 grams) kosher salt
- ¼ cup (57 grams) unsalted butter
- ¼ cup (60 grams) water
- ¼ cup (60 grams) whole milk
- ½ teaspoon vanilla extract
- 1 large egg (50 grams), room temperature

Filling:

- ⅓ cup (64 grams) chopped 66% cacao dark chocolate
- 3 tablespoons (42 grams) unsalted butter
- ¼ cup (30 grams) confectioners' sugar
- 3 tablespoons (15 grams) Dutch process cocoa powder
- ½ teaspoon kosher salt
- ⅓ cup (50 grams) finely chopped 66% cacao dark chocolate

- 1 large egg (50 grams)
- 2 tablespoons (30 grams) water, divided
- 1½ tablespoons (18 grams) granulated sugar

1. For dough: In the bowl of a stand mixer, whisk together 1 cup (125 grams) flour, granulated sugar, yeast, and salt by hand.
2. In a small saucepan, heat butter, ¼ cup (60 grams) water, milk, and vanilla over medium-low heat until an instant-read thermometer registers 120°F (49°C) to 130°F (54°C). Add hot butter mixture to flour mixture; using the paddle attachment, beat at medium-low speed until combined. Add room temperature egg, and beat until combined. With mixer on low speed, gradually add 1½ cups (188 grams) flour, beating just until combined and stopping to scrape sides of bowl.
3. Switch to the dough hook attachment. Beat at low speed until a soft, somewhat sticky dough forms, 5 to 7 minutes, stopping to scrape dough hook and sides of bowl; add up to remaining 2 tablespoons (16 grams) flour, 1 tablespoon (8 grams) at a time, if dough is too sticky. Turn out dough onto a very lightly floured surface, and shape into a smooth round.
4. Lightly oil a large bowl. Place dough in bowl, turning to grease top. Cover and let rise in a warm, draft-free place (75°F/24°C) until doubled in size, 30 to 45 minutes.
5. Turn out dough onto a very lightly floured surface, and gently press into an 8x6-inch rectangle. Loosely wrap with plastic wrap. Refrigerate for at least 1 hour or up to overnight.
6. For filling: In the top of a double boiler, melt chopped chocolate and butter over medium-low heat, stirring occasionally, until smooth and combined. Remove from heat. Whisk in confectioners' sugar, cocoa, and salt until smooth. Let cool to room temperature.
7. Spray an 8½x4½-inch loaf pan with cooking spray. Line pan with parchment paper, letting excess extend over sides of pan.
8. On a lightly floured surface, roll dough into a 13x10-inch rectangle (about ¼ inch thick). Using a small offset spatula, spread cooled cocoa mixture onto dough, leaving a ½-inch border on both short sides and one long side. Sprinkle with finely chopped chocolate onto cocoa mixture.
9. Starting with long side opposite border, roll up dough into a log, and pinch seam to seal. Gently lift log at each end, and stretch to 14 inches long. Place seam side down, making sure seam is off to one side instead of in center.
10. Using a sharp serrated knife, cut in half lengthwise. Turn halves cut side up, and place in an "X." Twist top half of "X" two times; pinch ends, and tuck under. Repeat with bottom half of "X." Using your hands, place in prepared pan, making sure to keep cut sides up and ends tucked. Cover and let rise in a warm, draft-free place (75°F/24°C) until puffed, 30 minutes to 1 hour. (Dough should pass the finger dent test; see page 17.)
11. Preheat oven to 350°F (180°C).

12. In a small bowl, whisk together egg and 1 tablespoon (15 grams) water; brush onto dough.
13. Bake until golden brown and an instant-read thermometer inserted in center registers 190°F (88°C), 45 to 50 minutes, covering with foil to prevent excess browning, if necessary.
14. Meanwhile, in a small microwave-safe bowl, heat granulated sugar and remaining 1 tablespoon (15 grams) water on high in 15-second intervals, stirring between each, until sugar dissolves. Let cool to room temperature before using.
15. Brush syrup onto hot babka, and let cool in pan for 10 minutes. Using excess parchment as handles, remove from pan, and let cool completely on a wire rack. Store in an airtight container for up to 3 days.

Babka Shaping 101

Keep a ruler on hand to check your dimensions, as anything less or more than this 13x10-inch rectangle will keep your babka from fitting the pan.

Spread filling onto dough, leaving a border, and sprinkle finely chopped chocolate on top. When you roll up the dough into a tight spiral, this border will allow the dough to form an airtight seal.

Starting with long side opposite border, roll up dough into a log, and pinch seam to seal. If you're having trouble closing the seam, simply wet the seam with some water and pinch together with your fingers. The water will help create a stickier surface on the dough so the seam holds.

Gently lift log at each end, and stretch to 14 inches long. This will help make your internal spiral nice and tight. Place seam side down, making sure seam is off to one side instead of in center.

Using a sharp serrated knife, cut in half lengthwise. Use a sharp serrated knife for cutting because its jagged edges cut through the roll more easily without pushing out the filling.

Turn halves cut side up, and place in an "X." Creating the "X" shape will help you make even twists on both sides, yielding a symmetrical loaf.

Twist top half of "X" two times; pinch ends, and tuck under. Repeat with bottom half of "X." Twisting on one side and then the other keeps you from having to twist two long, heavy strands. Instead, you're working with manageable shorter strands of dough, which will help keep the filling from falling out and your dough from being overworked.

Place in prepared pan, making sure to keep cut sides up and ends tucked. If you fail to tuck the ends, they'll pop up during baking and mar your beautiful shape.

Citrus-Poppy Seed Twists

Makes 10 buns

For a twist on the classic lemon-poppy seed pairing, orange and grapefruit unite to create an irresistible new combination. With soft, orange-scented dough and a sweet filling of poppy seeds and citrus zest, each intricate twist is sure to be a showstopper.

5¼ to 5½ cups (657 to 688 grams) all-purpose flour, divided
1¾ cups (350 grams) granulated sugar, divided
2¼ teaspoons (7 grams) instant yeast
1½ teaspoons kosher salt, divided
1 tablespoon (15 grams) plus 1 teaspoon tightly packed orange zest, divided
1 cup (240 grams) whole milk
1¼ cups (283 grams) unsalted butter, softened and divided
3 large eggs (150 grams), room temperature and divided
½ teaspoon vanilla extract
¼ cup (36 grams) poppy seeds
2 tablespoons (30 grams) tightly packed grapefruit zest
1 tablespoon (15 grams) water
1 cup (120 grams) confectioners' sugar
2 tablespoons (30 grams) fresh orange juice

1. In the bowl of a stand mixer, whisk together 4¾ cups (594 grams) flour, ¾ cup (150 grams) granulated sugar, yeast, 1 teaspoon kosher salt, and 1 teaspoon orange zest by hand until combined.
2. In a small saucepan, heat milk and ½ cup (113 grams) butter over medium heat until butter is melted and an instant-read thermometer registers 120°F (49°C) to 130°F (54°C). Add hot milk mixture to flour mixture; using the paddle attachment, beat at low speed until combined. Add 2 eggs (100 grams) and vanilla; beat until a wet, shaggy dough forms.
3. Switch to the dough hook attachment. Beat at medium-low speed until dough is smooth and elastic, 12 to 15 minutes; add up to ¼ cup (31 grams) flour, 1 tablespoon (8 grams) at a time, if dough is too sticky. Turn out dough onto a lightly floured surface, and knead 5 to 8 times; shape into a smooth round.
4. Lightly oil a large bowl. Place dough in bowl, turning to grease top. Cover and let rise in a warm, draft-free place (75°F/24°C) until doubled in size, 45 minutes to 1 hour.
5. In a small bowl, whisk together poppy seeds, remaining ½ cup (63 grams) flour, and remaining ½ teaspoon salt.
6. Clean bowl of stand mixer and paddle attachment. Using the paddle attachment, beat grapefruit zest, remaining 1 cup (200 grams) granulated sugar, remaining ¾ cup (170 grams) butter, and remaining 1 tablespoon (15 grams) orange zest at medium speed until combined, about 2 minutes. Beat in poppy seed mixture until just combined.
7. Line 2 rimmed baking sheets with parchment paper.
8. Punch down dough, and let stand for 10 minutes. Divide dough into 10 portions (about 120 grams each). On a clean surface, roll each portion into an 8x5-inch rectangle, with one long side closest to you. Spread about 3 tablespoons (45 grams) grapefruit zest mixture onto each rectangle, leaving a ¼-inch border along one long side. Starting with long side opposite border, roll up each rectangle into a log, pinching seam to seal. Place 1 log seam side down, and cut in half lengthwise. Pinch one end together, and twist halves together, cut side up. Pinch remaining end, and tie in a knot, tucking ends under each other. Repeat with remaining logs. Place about 2 inches apart on prepared pans. Cover and let rise in a warm, draft-free place (75°F/24°C) until puffy, about 45 minutes.
9. Preheat oven to 350°F (180°C).
10. In another small bowl, whisk together 1 tablespoon (15 grams) water and remaining 1 egg (50 grams). Lightly brush onto each bun.
11. Bake until puffed and golden brown and an instant-read thermometer inserted in center registers 190°F (88°C), 30 to 33 minutes. Let cool on pans for 10 minutes. Remove from pans, and let cool completely on a wire rack.
12. In another small bowl, whisk together confectioners' sugar and orange juice until smooth. Drizzle onto cooled buns. Best served same day.

Pan de Muerto

Makes 1 loaf

This traditional Mexican sweet bread is commonly made for Día de los Muertos (Day of the Dead) celebrations as a gift to the dearly departed. *Pan de muerto*—"bread of the dead"—is shaped into a round boule with strips of dough shaped and arranged on top to resemble the bones of the deceased. Under the glistening sugar-coated crust lies a pillowy bread perfumed with orange and anise seed and enticing enough to call forth the souls of the dead.

½ cup (120 grams) warm water (110°F/43°C to 115°F/46°C)
⅓ cup (67 grams) plus 3 tablespoons (36 grams) plus 1 teaspoon granulated sugar, divided
2¼ teaspoons (7 grams) instant yeast
1 tablespoon (10 grams) tightly packed orange zest
3¼ cups (413 grams) bread flour, divided
2½ teaspoons (8 grams) kosher salt
2 teaspoons (4 grams) anise seed
2 large eggs (100 grams), room temperature
2 teaspoons (8 grams) vanilla extract
1 teaspoon orange blossom water
6 tablespoons (84 grams) unsalted butter, room temperature
1 tablespoon (14 grams) unsalted butter, melted

1. In a medium bowl, whisk together ½ cup (120 grams) warm water, 1 teaspoon sugar, and yeast. Let stand until foamy, about 5 minutes.
2. In the bowl of a stand mixer, place ⅓ cup (67 grams) sugar; add orange zest, and rub zest into sugar until fragrant and well combined. Add 1½ cups (191 grams) flour, salt, and anise seed; using the paddle attachment, beat at low speed until combined.
3. Add eggs, one at a time, to yeast mixture, whisking until well combined after each addition. Whisk in vanilla and orange blossom water. Add yeast mixture to flour mixture, and beat at low speed until well combined. Add remaining 1¾ cups (222 grams) flour, and beat until a shaggy dough forms and no dry spots remains.
4. Switch to the dough hook attachment. Beat at low speed until dough becomes smooth, elastic, and slightly tacky, 4 to 5 minutes. Add room temperature butter, 1 tablespoon (14 grams) at a time, beating until combined after each addition (5 to 6 minutes total). Beat until a smooth, elastic dough forms, 8 to 10 minutes. Turn out dough onto a clean surface, and shape into a smooth round.
5. Lightly oil a large bowl. Place dough in bowl, turning to grease top. Cover and let rise in a warm, draft-free place (75°F/24°C) until doubled in size, about 1 hour.
6. Line a baking sheet with parchment paper.
7. Lightly punch down dough. Cover and let stand for 5 minutes. Turn out dough onto a lightly floured surface, and cut off one-fourth of dough (about 200 grams). Reserve, and cover dough to prevent it from drying out.
8. Press remaining dough into a ½-inch-thick disk. Lift bottom edge of dough, and gently stretch and fold bottom third over center third. Stretch right side out, and fold over center third; repeat with left side. Finish by folding top third over previous folds. Roll dough away from you, and using both hands, cup dough and pull it toward you to seal. Rotate dough 90 degrees, and pull again, repeating until a tight, smooth boule forms. Place, seam side down, on prepared pan.
9. Divide reserved dough in half (about 100 grams each). Working with 1 portion at a time, roll into a 6½-inch-long log. In center of log (3¼ inches from either end), pinch dough, and roll with your fingers to form 2 smaller logs joined by a thin center. Measuring from center, in each direction, mark 1¾ inches. Pinch and roll at each mark to create 4 connected sections. Shape each section into a ball. Repeat with remaining reserved dough.
10. Place 1 strip of shaped dough across top of boule. Place second strip of shaped dough on boule perpendicular to first strip, crossing at the center. Cover and let rise in a warm, draft-free place (75°F/24°C) until almost doubled in size, 1 hour and 20 minutes to 1½ hours. (Dough should pass the finger dent test; see page 17.)
11. Preheat oven to 350°F (180°C).
12. Bake until golden brown and an instant-read thermometer inserted in center registers 190°F (88°C), 35 to 40 minutes, covering with foil after 15 to 20 minutes of baking to prevent excess browning. Remove from pan, and let cool on a wire rack for 30 minutes.
13. Brush melted butter onto bread; sprinkle with remaining 3 tablespoons (36 grams) sugar. Serve warm or at room temperature.

Swedish Buns

Makes 15 buns

Swedish cardamom buns called *kardemummabullar* are twisted breads infused with an aromatic butter-sugar-cardamom filling and topped with a fragrant flourish of more cardamom and sugar. Or you can fill the cardamom-infused dough with cinnamon, sugar, and butter for Swedish cinnamon buns, called *kanelbullar*, which are generously adorned with crunchy Swedish pearl sugar. Either way, they're best served warm with a cup of steaming coffee or tea, destined to brighten even the bleakest of winter days.

Dough:
3¾ cups (477 grams) bread flour, divided
¼ cup (50 grams) granulated sugar
2¼ teaspoons (7 grams) active dry yeast
2 teaspoons (6 grams) kosher salt
2 teaspoons (4 grams) freshly ground cardamom seeds (see Note)
1 cup (240 grams) whole milk
⅓ cup (76 grams) unsalted butter
1 large egg (50 grams), room temperature

Cinnamon filling (option 1):
¼ cup (57 grams) unsalted butter, room temperature
¼ cup (55 grams) firmly packed light brown sugar
2 tablespoons (16 grams) bread flour
2 teaspoons (4 grams) ground cinnamon
¼ teaspoon kosher salt

Cardamom filling (option 2):
½ cup (100 grams) granulated sugar
1 tablespoon (6 grams) freshly ground cardamom seeds (see Note)
¼ cup (57 grams) unsalted butter, room temperature
2 tablespoons (16 grams) bread flour
¼ teaspoon kosher salt

1 large egg (50 grams), room temperature
1 tablespoon (15 grams) water
Swedish pearl sugar, for sprinkling

1. For dough: In the bowl of a stand mixer fitted with the paddle attachment, beat 1½ cups (191 grams) flour, granulated sugar, yeast, salt, and cardamom at low speed just until combined.
2. In a medium saucepan, heat milk and butter over medium heat, stirring occasionally, until butter is melted and an instant-read thermometer registers 120°F (49°C) to 130°F (54°C). Add hot milk mixture to flour mixture; beat at medium speed until combined, 1 to 2 minutes. Add egg; beat at medium-high speed for 2 minutes. Gradually add remaining 2¼ cups (286 grams) flour, beating just until combined and stopping to scrape bottom and sides of bowl.
3. Switch to the dough hook attachment. Beat at medium-low speed until a soft, smooth, elastic dough forms, 6 to 10 minutes. (Dough may still stick slightly to sides of bowl but should pass the windowpane test; see page 16.) Turn out dough onto a clean surface, and shape into a round.
4. Oil a large bowl. Place dough in bowl, turning to grease top. Cover and let rise in a warm, draft-free place (75°F/24°C) until doubled in size, 45 minutes to 1 hour.
5. Punch down dough. On a clean surface, pat dough into a 10x6-inch rectangle. Wrap in plastic wrap, and refrigerate for at least 8 hours or up to overnight.
6. For cinnamon filling: In a medium bowl, stir together butter, brown sugar, flour, cinnamon, and salt until well combined.
7. Alternatively, for cardamom filling: In a small bowl, whisk together granulated sugar and cardamom; reserve ¼ cup (50 grams) cardamom sugar in a small bowl. Stir butter, flour, and salt into remaining cardamom sugar until well combined.
8. Let dough stand at room temperature for 5 minutes. On a lightly floured surface, roll dough into a 25x10-inch rectangle, with one long side closest to you. Using an offset spatula, dollop desired filling onto dough, and spread in a thin, even layer to edges. Working from short sides, fold dough in thirds like a letter.
9. Line 2 rimmed baking sheets with parchment paper.
10. Roll dough into an 11x8-inch rectangle, with one long side closest to you. Using a pastry wheel or sharp knife, cut dough lengthwise into 15 strips (about ¾ inch wide each). Holding up one end of 1 strip vertically, gently pull dough in increments until strip is 22 inches long, being careful to keep an even thickness throughout dough so it does not tear. Grabbing bottom

end of strip between index and middle fingers and thumb of one hand, loosely wrap dough strip three times around fingers of your other hand, overlapping dough slightly. Place thumb of same hand over overlapped dough to secure; wrap remaining end of dough perpendicularly, between index and middle fingers, and around overlapping dough to form a knot-like shape, tucking loose end under bottom of finished bun as you remove your fingers. Repeat with remaining strips, and place about 2 inches apart on prepared pans.
11. Cover and let rise in a warm, draft-free place (75°F/24°C) until doubled in size and dough holds an indentation when gently pressed, 1 hour to 1½ hours.
12. Preheat oven to 350°F (180°C).
13. In another small bowl, whisk together egg and 1 tablespoon (15 grams) water; brush onto buns. Sprinkle with pearl sugar or reserved cardamom sugar as desired.
14. Bake until golden brown and an instant-read thermometer inserted in center registers at least 190°F (88°C), 15 to 20 minutes, rotating pans halfway through baking. Immediately sprinkle with additional pearl sugar or any remaining reserved cardamom sugar, if desired. Let cool on pans for 5 minutes. Serve warm. Store in an airtight container for up to 2 days.

Note: *I used freshly ground cardamom seeds. For store-bought ground cardamom, use 1¾ teaspoons (3 grams) ground cardamom in the dough and 4 teaspoons (8 grams) ground cardamom in the cardamom filling.*

Swedish Bun Shaping 101

Letting the dough stand at room temperature for a few minutes allows it to relax a little so it's easier to roll it out.

Dotting the surface of the dough with small mounds of the filling and gently spreading all over the surface helps you achieve a perfect, even layer.

Making small notches at ¾-inch intervals gives you a guide to follow to continue cutting the strips of dough.

If you can't pull the strips long enough without the dough springing back, cover with a kitchen towel, let stand for 10 minutes, and then return to it.

Keeping the shaping loose is key! A loose knot gives the dough space to proof and expand before baking. Too tight, and the strain against itself will cause the bun to unravel.

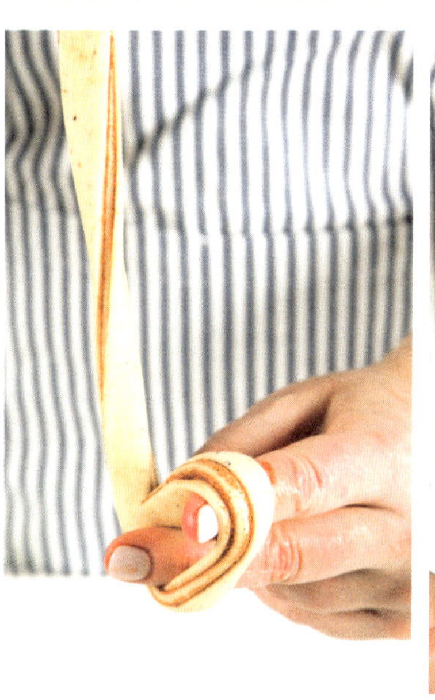

The egg wash gives the buns a gloriously golden exterior and helps the cardamom sugar topping or the Swedish pearl sugar stick to the dough.

Peanut Butter-Banana Braid

Makes 1 loaf

Elegant but packing the homey, nostalgic flavor of peanut butter and banana, this braid is the perfect way to enjoy something classic in a gorgeous new package.

Dough:
3 cups (382 grams) bread flour, divided
3 tablespoons (36 grams) granulated sugar
2½ teaspoons (8 grams) kosher salt
2¼ teaspoons (7 grams) active dry yeast
½ cup (120 grams) whole milk
¼ cup (57 grams) unsalted butter
¼ cup (60 grams) water
2 teaspoons (8 grams) vanilla extract
1 large egg (50 grams), room temperature

Filling:
¼ cup (57 grams) unsalted butter, softened
⅓ cup (73 grams) firmly packed light brown sugar
⅓ cup (85 grams) creamy peanut butter
½ cup (100 grams) chopped banana

1 large egg (50 grams)
1 tablespoon (15 grams) water
Garnish: confectioners' sugar

1. For dough: In the bowl of a stand mixer fitted with the paddle attachment, combine 1½ cups (191 grams) flour, granulated sugar, salt, and yeast.
2. In a medium saucepan, heat milk, butter, ¼ cup (60 grams) water, and vanilla over medium heat until an instant-read thermometer registers 120°F (49°C) to 130°F (54°C). Add hot milk mixture to flour mixture, and beat at medium speed until combined. Beat in room temperature egg. With mixer on low speed, gradually add remaining 1½ cups (191 grams) flour, beating just until combined and stopping to scrape sides of bowl.
3. Switch to the dough hook attachment. Beat at low speed until a soft, somewhat sticky dough forms, 6 to 7 minutes, stopping to scrape dough hook and sides of bowl. (Dough will be elastic and pull away from sides of bowl but stick to bottom of bowl.) Turn out dough onto a lightly floured surface, and shape into a smooth round.
4. Lightly oil a large bowl. Place dough in bowl, turning to grease top. Cover and let rise in a warm, draft-free place (75°F/24°C) until almost doubled in size, 45 minutes to 1 hour.
5. Punch down dough, and let stand for 5 minutes.
6. For filling: In a medium bowl, beat butter and brown sugar with a mixer at medium speed until fluffy, 1 to 2 minutes, stopping to scrape sides of bowl. Add peanut butter, and beat just until combined.
7. Turn out dough onto a lightly floured sheet of parchment paper. Roll into a 16x10-inch oval. Using a small knife or bench scraper, score or mark a 13x4-inch rectangle in center of dough, leaving a 1½-inch border on short sides and a 3-inch border on long sides.
8. Spread peanut butter mixture onto dough in rectangle; top with banana. Cut 1-inch-wide strips along each side of filling. At top and bottom, trim ends to width of filling, and fold over filling.
9. Starting on left side, stretch, twist, and fold top strip over filling, ending just below opposite top strip. Repeat with top strip on right side. Continue pattern, alternating left and right, until you reach end of strips. Tuck and pinch last strip. (If dough is not sticking to itself, dab with a little water to help it seal.) Transfer dough, on parchment, to a baking sheet. Cover and let rise in a warm, draft-free place (75°F/24°C) until puffed, 30 to 45 minutes.
10. Preheat oven to 350°F (180°C).
11. In a small bowl, whisk together egg and 1 tablespoon (15 grams) water; brush onto dough.
12. Bake until golden brown and an instant-read thermometer inserted in bread (not filling) registers 190°F (88°C), 20 to 25 minutes. Let cool for 15 to 20 minutes. Garnish with confectioners' sugar, if desired. Best served warm. Refrigerate in an airtight container for up to 2 days.

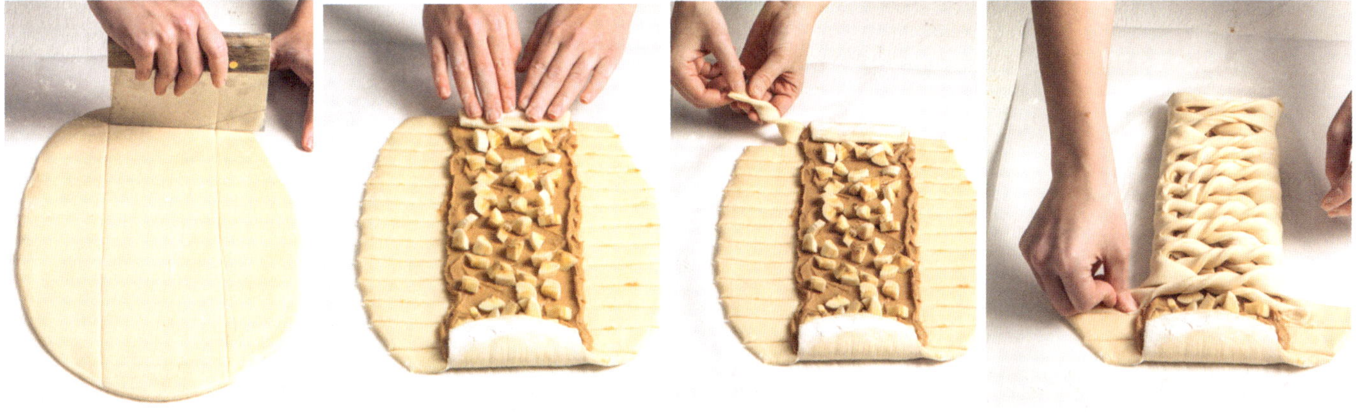

Blueberry-Lemon Cream Cheese Star Bread

Makes 1 (14-inch) loaf

Like the dramatic Tarte Soleil (page 176), this bread is shaped by cutting a filled round of dough into wedges that remain attached at the center. Each segment is twisted outward, creating a radiant sunburst pattern. As it bakes, the twists form crisp golden ridges while the center stays soft and tender—perfect for pulling apart and sharing.

Dough:
3¼ cups plus 2 tablespoons (422 grams) all-purpose flour, divided
¼ cup (50 grams) granulated sugar
2¼ teaspoons (7 grams) instant yeast
2 teaspoons (6 grams) kosher salt
1 cup (240 grams) whole milk
¼ cup (57 grams) unsalted butter, softened
1 large egg (50 grams), room temperature
2 teaspoons (12 grams) vanilla bean paste

Filling:
4 ounces (113 grams) cream cheese, softened
¼ cup (30 grams) confectioners' sugar
¼ cup (9 grams) freeze-dried blueberries, finely crushed*
1 tablespoon (3 grams) lemon zest
1 tablespoon (15 grams) lightly beaten egg white
¼ teaspoon ground cardamom

1 large egg (50 grams), room temperature
1 tablespoon (15 grams) water
Sparkling sugar, for sprinkling
Cream Cheese Glaze (recipe on page 144)

1. For dough: In the bowl of a stand mixer fitted with the paddle attachment, beat 1 cup (125 grams) flour, granulated sugar, yeast, and salt at medium-low speed until well combined, stopping to scrape sides of bowl.
2. In a medium saucepan, heat milk and butter over medium heat until an instant-read thermometer registers 120°F (49°C) to 130°F (54°C). Add hot milk mixture to flour mixture; beat at medium speed for 2 minutes, stopping to scrape sides of bowl. Add egg and vanilla bean paste; beat at medium-high speed for 2 minutes.
3. With mixer on low speed, gradually add remaining 2¼ cups plus 2 tablespoons (297 grams) flour, beating just until combined and stopping to scrape sides of bowl.
4. Switch to the dough hook attachment. Beat at medium speed until a soft, somewhat sticky dough forms, 6 to 8 minutes, stopping to scrape dough hook and sides of bowl. (Dough should pass the windowpane test but may still stick slightly to sides of bowl; see page 16.)
5. Spray a large bowl with cooking spray. Place dough in bowl, turning to grease top. Cover and let rise in a warm, draft-free place (75°F/24°C) until doubled in size, 40 minutes to 1 hour.
6. Lightly punch down dough; cover and let stand for 5 minutes.
7. Line a 17½x12½-inch light-colored rimmed baking sheet with parchment paper.
8. Turn out dough, and divide into 4 portions (about 200 grams each); gently shape each into a ball. Cover with plastic wrap, and let stand for 15 minutes.
9. For filling: In a small bowl, stir together cream cheese, confectioners' sugar, blueberries, lemon zest, egg white, and cardamom until well combined.
10. Keeping other portions covered with plastic wrap, roll and pat 1 dough ball into an 11-inch circle; gently place on prepared pan. (Dough may shrink slightly.) Spread one-third of filling (about 3½ tablespoons or 55 grams) onto dough circle, leaving a ½-inch border around edges. Repeat with 2 dough balls and remaining filling, stacking layers. Roll remaining dough ball into an 11-inch circle, and place on top of previous layers.
11. Place a 1½-inch round cutter in center of dough; gently press down just to leave a mark. Using a sharp knife or a pizza wheel, make 16 evenly spaced cuts from center mark to edge of dough. Grasping 1 cut piece in each hand, twist pieces away from each other twice; firmly pinch ends together to adhere. Repeat with remaining cut pieces. Cover and let rise in a warm, draft-free place (75°F/24°C) until nearly doubled in size, 30 to 45 minutes.
12. Preheat oven to 375°F (190°C).

13. In another small bowl, whisk together egg and 1 tablespoon (15 grams) water; brush onto dough, and sprinkle with sparkling sugar. Pinch ends together again, if necessary.

14. Bake until golden brown and an instant-read thermometer inserted in center registers at least 190°F (88°C), 16 to 22 minutes, loosely covering with foil to prevent excess browning, if necessary. Let cool completely on pan on a wire rack.

15. Just before serving, drizzle Cream Cheese Glaze onto bread. Refrigerate in an airtight container for up to 3 days.

**To finely crush whole freeze-dried blueberries, place in a large resealable plastic bag and pound with a rolling pin.*

Sweet Custard Wool Bread

Makes 1 (8-inch) loaf

Break out your springform pan to bake the most photo-worthy sweet bread of the season. With a custard filling made irresistible with sweetened condensed milk, this incredibly fluffy, enriched yeast bread gets its rippled "wooly" appearance with a simple cut-and-roll technique.

Custard:

6 tablespoons (90 grams) whole milk
5 tablespoons (100 grams) sweetened condensed milk, divided
2 large egg yolks (37 grams), room temperature
1 tablespoon (8 grams) cornstarch
¼ teaspoon kosher salt
1 tablespoon (14 grams) unsalted butter, softened
¼ teaspoon vanilla bean paste

Tangzhong:

¼ cup (60 grams) whole milk
1½ tablespoons (12 grams) bread flour

Dough:

2¼ to 2½ cups (286 to 318 grams) bread flour, divided
2 tablespoons (24 grams) granulated sugar
2 teaspoons (6 grams) kosher salt
2 teaspoons (6 grams) instant yeast
¼ cup (60 grams) water
¼ cup (60 grams) whole milk
3 tablespoons (42 grams) unsalted butter, softened
1 tablespoon (19 grams) sweetened condensed milk
1 large egg (50 grams), room temperature

1 large egg (50 grams)
1 tablespoon (15 grams) water

1. For custard: In a small saucepan, whisk together whole milk and 2½ tablespoons (50 grams) condensed milk. Cook over medium heat, stirring frequently, until steaming. (Do not boil.)
2. In a medium bowl, whisk together egg yolks, cornstarch, salt, and remaining 2½ tablespoons (50 grams) condensed milk. Gradually whisk warm milk mixture into egg yolk mixture. Pour egg yolk mixture into saucepan. Cook over medium heat, whisking frequently, until very thick, like a pudding, 3 to 5 minutes.
3. Strain custard through a fine-mesh sieve into a medium heatproof bowl, discarding solids. Whisk in butter and vanilla bean paste until well combined. Cover with plastic wrap, pressing wrap directly onto surface of custard to prevent a skin from forming. Refrigerate until thick and cold, at least 2 hours, or up to overnight. Stir until smooth before using.
4. For tangzhong: In a small saucepan, whisk together milk and flour. Cook over medium-low heat, whisking constantly, until thickened, whisk leaves lines on bottom of pan, and an instant-read thermometer registers 149°F (65°C). Transfer to a small bowl, and let cool completely.
5. For dough: In the bowl of a stand mixer fitted with the paddle attachment, beat 1 cup (127 grams) flour, sugar, salt, and yeast at medium-low speed just until combined.
6. In a medium saucepan, heat ¼ cup (60 grams) water, whole milk, and butter over medium heat, stirring frequently, until butter is melted and an instant-read thermometer registers 120°F (49°C) to 130°F (54°C). Add hot milk mixture and condensed milk to flour mixture; beat at medium-low speed until combined, 30 seconds to 1 minute, stopping to scrape sides of bowl. Add cooled tangzhong and room temperature egg; beat until combined, 30 seconds to 1 minute. With mixer on low speed, gradually add 1¼ cups (159 grams) flour, beating just until combined.
7. Switch to the dough hook attachment. Beat at medium-low speed until a soft, smooth, slightly tacky dough forms, 5 to 9 minutes, stopping to scrape dough hook and sides of bowl; add up to remaining ¼ cup (32 grams) flour, 1 tablespoon (8 grams) at a time, if dough is too sticky. (Dough should pass the windowpane test; see page 16.) Turn out dough onto a clean surface, and gently shape into a ball.
8. Spray a large bowl with cooking spray. Place dough in bowl, turning to grease top. Cover and let rise in a warm, draft-free place (75°F/24°C) until doubled in size, 40 minutes to 1 hour.
9. Punch down dough; cover and let stand for 10 minutes.
10. On a clean surface, divide dough into 5 portions (about 118 grams each). Roll each portion into a ball, pinching any seams closed if needed. Cover and let stand for 15 minutes.

11. Generously spray an 8-inch light-colored metal springform pan with baking spray with flour. Line bottom of pan with parchment paper.
12. On a clean surface, place 1 dough ball smooth side down, and roll into a 10x5-inch oval (about ⅛ inch thick). Starting about 5½ inches from one short end of oval, using a greased pizza cutter or sharp knife, cut remaining dough lengthwise into ⅛-inch-wide strands. (It will look like there is fringe on one side of oval.)
13. Stir cooled custard; spread about 1 tablespoon (about 32 grams) custard onto solid side of dough, leaving a ¼- to ½-inch border around edge. Fold sides of oval ¼ to ½ inch over filling. Starting on short end opposite dough fringe, roll up dough into a log shape. Place, seam side down, against sides of prepared pan.
14. Repeat with remaining dough and remaining custard, placing dough logs end to end around sides of pan. (Gently push previous logs over to create room for new logs, if needed). Cover and let rise in a warm draft-free place (75°F/24°C) until doubled in size and dough holds an indentation when pressed, 40 minutes to 1 hour.
15. Preheat oven to 350°F (180°C).
16. In a small bowl, whisk together egg and 1 tablespoon (15 grams) water; brush onto dough.
17. Bake until golden brown and an instant-read thermometer inserted near center (in bread, not filling) registers at least 190°F (88°C), 24 to 30 minutes, rotating pan halfway through baking and loosely covering with foil after 20 minutes of baking to prevent excess browning. Let cool in pan for 10 minutes. Using a sharp knife or small offset spatula, carefully loosen bread from sides of pan. Remove sides of pan; let cool completely on pan base on a wire rack before serving. Store in an airtight container for up to 3 days.

Wool Bread Shaping 101

Roll 1 dough ball into a 10x5-inch oval (about ⅛ inch thick).

Starting about 5½ inches from one short end of oval (lightly score the 5½-inch mark to make things easier), cut dough lengthwise into ⅛-inch-wide strands. It will look like there is fringe on one side of oval.

Spread about 1 tablespoon (about 32 grams) custard onto solid side of dough, leaving a ¼- to ½-inch border around edge.

Fold sides of oval ¼ to ½ inch over filling.

Starting on short end opposite dough fringe, roll up dough into a log shape.

Place, seam side down, against sides of prepared pan. Repeat with remaining dough and remaining custard, placing dough logs end to end around sides of pan.

index

Editor-in-Chief Brian Hart Hoffman
EVP/Chief Content Officer Brooke Michael Bell
Contributing Editor Nancy Meeks
Senior Features Editor Amber Wilson

Assistant Editor Shelby Duffy
Baking and Pastry Editor Katie Moon
Senior Copy Editor, Food Meg Lundberg

Art Director Liz Kight
Senior Digital Imaging Specialist Delisa McDaniel
Graphic Designer Courtney Bell

Test Kitchen Director Laura Crandall
Recipe Developers/ Food Stylists Ola Agbodza, Katie Moon, Amanda Stabile, Giovanna Vazquez

Photographers Jim Bathie, Katie Graves, John O'Hagan, Stephanie Welbourne Steele

Cover Photography by Stephanie Welbourne Steele
Food styling by Katie Moon

about the author

A former flight attendant and self-taught baker, Brian Hart Hoffman spent his early life traveling and discovering bakeries around the world, returning home with a mission to re-create the recipes. Brian launched an award-winning brand dedicated to the celebration of the global baking community: Bake from Scratch. Now, Bake from Scratch is one of the world's largest baking platforms, with magazines and best-selling cookbooks, sell-out international and domestic baking retreats, and, of course, @thebakefeed on Instagram, a way for bakers around the world to connect.

Brian has authored numerous best-selling books, including *The Coupe, Holiday Coupetails, Every Day Coupetails, Fast-Fix Baking, The Bread Collection, The Cake Collection, The Pie & Tart Collection, The Cookie Collection, The Bundt Collection, Another Bundt Collection, Holiday Cookies, It's Time to Bake Pastries,* and *Bake from Scratch: Artisan Recipes for the Home Baker* volumes 1–10.